Circling and Authentic Relating Practice Guide

Marc Bénéteau

"If we were all to sit in a circle and confess our sins, we would laugh at each other for lack of originality" — Kahlil Gibran

Copyright © 2017 Marc Bénéteau. Self-published on CreateSpace and at http://CirclingGuide.com

ISBN: 197583402X

Quotes by Bryan Bayer, Sara Ness, Decker Cunov, Alexis Shepperd and others. Contributions by Daniel Tenner, Andrea Zwingel, Shirley Norwood, Ryan Schoenbeck, Andrew McDonald and others. Cover design by Jim Hayes (http://www.ha-yesdesign.com/).

With gratitude to my many mentors, in particular Jerry Jud, Victor Baranco, Werner Erhard, Marshall Rosenberg, and Dieter Duhm. I rest on the shoulders of giants.

Contents

FOREWORD 6
PREFACE: MY STORY 7
CHAPTER 1: WHAT IS CIRCLING? 10
    What is Circling? 10
    Why a book about Circling? 10
    Circling in a nutshell: the goal of Circling 11
    Logistics of Circling 13
    Why Circle? 14
    History of Circling 16
    Organization of this book 20
CHAPTER 2: CIRCLING BASIC CONCEPTS 21
    What is Circling, really? 21
    Formal Circling vs. "Guerrilla Circling" 22
CHAPTER 3: CIRCLING BEST PRACTICES 24
    Notice feelings and body sensations 24
    Connect with the group – up to a point (follow your aliveness) .. 25
    Get Their World: Lead from Attention, Curiosity, and Empathy 27
    Validate and Appreciate 30
    Lead from Vulnerability 33
    Share Impact, Offer Reflection and Inquiry 37
    Own Your Experience (Communicate Responsibly) 43
    Make Right, Not Wrong (Find People Right, Approve of them). 46
    Be Impactable 47
    Honor Yourself (Handling Conflict) 48
    Welcome Everything 51
    Slow Down 53
    Surrender Gracefully 54
    Conclusion 55
CHAPTER 4: CIRCLING PERSPECTIVES AND ADVANCED PRACTICES 56
    Circling, Integral Theory, and the AQAL model 56
    Surrendered Leadership and "We space" 58
    Circling in Business 59
    The Yin and Yang of Circling: Connection Intent versus Developmental Intent 60

Topical Circling 62
CHAPTER 5: COMPLEMENTARY MODALITIES 64
Non-Violent Communication 64
Authentic Man Program and Authentic Woman Experience 66
The Avalon Community 67
Circling, Mental Health / Addiction Recovery, and Functional Medicine 68
Self-Circling, Circling Europe style 69
Self-Circling, IFS / IRF style 70
Inner-Relationship Focusing (Ann Weiser Cornell) 72
Withholds, Victor Baranco style 72
Withholds, Boulder Integral style 75
Network For a New Culture and ZEGG 76
Somatic Experiencing and Hakomi 78
Adult Attachment Theory 79
The Evolutionary Relationships Movement (Patricia Albere) 80
Sociocracy 81
Other compatible modalities 81

CHAPTER 6: NEXT STEPS 83
Facilitation of Circles, and Running Private Circles 84
Please join the Circling Guide community! 85

ARTICLES AND STORIES 86
What is authenticity? (Sara Ness) 86
Beyond Circling: I have a dream (Marc Beneteau) 89
Selling Authentic Relating, Part 2 (Marc Beneteau) 93

RESOURCES 97
Training Organizations 97
Online Circling 98
Books, articles and podcasts about Circling 99
Differences in the various schools of Circling 99

LEADER FORMATS 103
Summary of the Leader Formats 103
Overall leadership guidelines 103
A/R Game Format 105
Circling Introduction Leader Format 109
Overall Leadership Guidelines 109

TIPS FOR GIVING AND RECEIVING FEEDBACK 113
  Why giving feedback is important 113
  Tips for giving feedback 114
  Tips for receiving feedback 114
OTHER BOOKS BY MARC 116
  As Lovers Do: Sexual and Romantic Partnership as a Path of Transformation 116

FOREWORD

"No one cares how much you know, until they know how much you care" – Theodore Roosevelt

This book fulfills three deep desires of mine.

My first desire was to write a practice guide to Circling that could be read in one sitting and give the essence of the modality. A guide that might be especially useful to those of us with short attention spans.

My second desire was to share my excitement about the Authentic Relating movement, which has been so fun and so transformational for me in such a short time, in the hope of inspiring others to try it out for themselves.

And my third desire was to put Circling into the context where I think it squarely belongs: as a revolutionary practice aimed at extending the reach of loving kindness in the world. As such there is no sphere of life, public or private, that cannot benefit from the skills described here. You can practice Authentic Relating (A/R) with anyone, whether they are aware of your intentions or not, and **if you do it correctly (which is not always easy) it is very likely that you will get *phenomenal* results with most people.**

I am currently traveling throughout the US and Europe, looking for opportunities to bring Circling and Surrendered Leadership practices into the world in three particular areas that I am very passionate about: the intentional community / eco-village movement, mental health and addiction recovery, and sexuality. If you are interested in these topics and want to support me or share resources, write to me at marc@CirclingGuide.com

Finally: I am grateful for any corrections, feedback (positive or negative), and inspirational stories.

With love,
Marc

PREFACE: MY STORY

> *"The true test of your spiritual success is the happiness of the people around you"* – Swami Rudrananda (Rudi)

In 1985, at the age of 25, I found myself after a relationship breakup in a deep and chemically-resistant depression. It was the most painful thing that had ever happened to me, and it completely shocked me. I was at the time, as many men in our culture, entirely cut-off from my feelings and lacking even a rudimentary understanding of emotional communication.

In a bold and naïve move, traits which have followed me my entire life, I dropped out of my engineering program and moved to California, the epicenter of the human potential movement, in order to "find myself". I decided then, in that terrible but ultimately redeeming moment, that the only thing that truly interested me was human relationships, and that if I were to have a life that would be successful in my own eyes, it would need to be principally focused on learning and teaching love – despite feeling that I had begun my life virtually retarded in those skills. This lifestyle decision was confirmed later, after I read Dale Carnegie (in How to Win Friends and Influence People), and realized that in a complex and inter-related world, the skills of human relationship are fundamental to the achievement of even traditional forms of success, such as wealth and power.

Over the next 30 years, I intensively explored what I call the "marketplace of love". I read every book, enrolled in every form of therapy, every type of community-based healing group, every Large Group Awareness Training (LGAT) and every New Religious Movement (NRM) which I could find and which my financial resources allowed (and in those days my resources were considerable). I discovered that the search for love and community is fraught with perils: delusions, projections, and ego inflation. In many of the groups that I explored I had a real sense of "coming home", that I had found what I was seeking, and in too many cases, later discovered serious ethical problems ranging from abuses of power, inappropriate sexual behavior, or excessive profit motive.

I did find two movements which particularly moved me and which were in integrity. One was Buddhism, which is actually more of a practical psychology than a religion; and the other was Non-Violent Communication (NVC), in which I discovered a number of very valuable distinctions relating to human relationships as well as a practice community. In 2007 I got married and founded an intentional community with my wife, which we designed as an "experimental community of love in action", and ran quite successfully for 3 years. Those were the happiest years of my life up to that point. And then, our community was shut-down by the municipality over zoning issues, my marriage fell apart, and I was back to square one. Kahlil Gibran was right: the ways of love are hard and steep, indeed.

Finally, in 2014 I discovered Circling, and in 2016 moved to Boulder, Colorado, and joined the Integral Center there. Very rapidly I found myself inside an active, loving and engaged community, forming friendships which I believe will last my entire life, and having powerful insights and experiences daily. I felt that this was the developmental community that I had been seeking my whole life, another instance of an experimental community of love in action. What made the offer even more compelling was that the groups were very low-cost, thereby holding the promise of what I call "the democratization of transformation", another goal of mine; and finally, the distributed organizational structure reduced the danger of the kinds of abuses which plague these types of movements, as well as creating more diversity.

I could hardly believe my good luck. Feeling compelled to write about it, I did so, while imagining that the book would be read and that it would have an impact. What you have in your hands is the result. The two previous books, by Bryan Bayer and Sara Ness, are at least as good. I still wanted to bring in my voice, insights gathered over 30 years of research in building community, emotional communication and the psychology of love. You will also find here an up-to-date history of the Authentic Relating movement and an extensive Resources section.

I offer this in gratitude to the pioneers of the Authentic Relating movement: Guy Sengstock, Decker Cunov, Bryan Bayer, Alexis

Shepperd, Robert McNaughton, Sean Wilkinson, John Thompson, Sara Ness, Jordan Allen, Shana James, Amy Silverman, and others. You are my heroes!

As an "open source", community-generated practice, Circling will continue to evolve and deepen, even to a degree far beyond what I am attempting to contextualize here.

CHAPTER 1: WHAT IS CIRCLING?

> *"Along with chocolate, sex and samadhi, Circling is best experienced directly"* – Bryan Bayer, author of <u>The Art of Circling</u>
>
> *"If I am not for myself, then who will be for me? But if I am only for myself, who am I?"* – Hillel

What is Circling?

Circling is a group conversation practice that usually lasts an hour to an hour and a half, and involves 3 to 9 people. It is possible, however, to have it go on for days and to engage as many as 50 people or more. It also works well in pairs and it is even possible to do it alone (see "Self-Circling" below). Circling happens either in person in many places around the world, or via online web-conferencing technology (see the Resources section). Both are great. There are also weekend workshops and advanced training programs, which often run 6 to 9 months.

Why a book about Circling?

Often in a circle with beginners I hear some variation of this statement: *"I like what's going on here but I am not quite sure what is acceptable here, what is Okay for me to do or say."* When I hear this, I usually get happy, for two reasons. First because this expression is a significant **reveal** (an aspect of **leading with vulnerability**, which I will discuss more later), and as such opens up the possibility of a rich inquiry for the individual and for the group. And the second reason I get happy on hearing this, is because it is a profound question that can't be properly answered in a sound-bite. Indeed, it is a question that is at the very heart of creating deep, transformational human relationships, and as such is also at the core of the Circling inquiry: **When and how do we give to others, when and how do we receive from them, and when and how do we give to ourselves? What is really going on here between us?**

I wrote this book as an attempt to answer that fundamental question, the question that is at the heart of deep human connection, which in turn relates to the nature of love, the meaning of suffering, and the human journey to wholeness. Ultimately, that is the Circling inquiry.

I offer all this with an important caveat: as noted in Bryan's quote above, Circling, like love, can't be taught in a book. The successful *practice* of Circling is likely to be more enjoyable and more growthful than reading about it. Even so, a book can provide a **context** (of shared understanding, shared values) from which a powerful conversation is more likely to emerge.

Circling in a nutshell: the goal of Circling

Circling is, first and foremost, a practice of un-withheld present-moment connection to self and others. It is the attempt to understand what it's like to be in another person's skin, while simultaneously being true to ourselves. It's about seeing people for who they really are, "getting their world", and giving and receiving the kind of attention that changes lives and which allows new possibilities to emerge.

An alternative formulation would say that Circling is about discovering "truth", or about bringing more self-awareness and discernment into the experience of life, in order to cultivate connection with oneself and others. To note here (and we will return to this topic) that "cultivating connection" may involve the noticing and reporting of lack-of-connection.

As such, anything you say or do in a Circling group, or anything you withhold in a Circling group, ought to successfully pass this test: **is this intervention (or conscious decision to NOT intervene) serving connection?** Is it serving truth, is it serving the group, is it creating more aliveness in me or others?

Of course, we frequently make mistakes in judgment about whether a particular intervention and self-expression (or else a failure to express) is serving truth or connection. We may be silent when we should have spoken, or say the wrong thing, or say the right thing but poorly; or we can't come up with anything to say at all, we are so completely befuddled, or full of anger, grief or shame. And yet, we seem to be compelled to keep on trying to communicate and to connect. And hopefully, by allowing ourselves to make these mistakes and then witnessing the impact, we get better at it.

This is the core Circling practice, in my understanding of it. If you have already experienced this degree of connection and of truth-telling (and most of us have, even briefly), then you know what to do, more or less, and you can read the rest of this book with a desire to refine and sharpen your current level of self-awareness and discrimination around this very fundamental question*:* **am I, in this moment, serving truth and connection, or am I doing the opposite (hiding, lying and creating distance)? Who am I being right now, and why?**

Two more distinctions here that might be helpful.

The first distinction is to acknowledge that while all aspects of our humanity are important – our beliefs and ideas, plans, "stories", needs and desires, etc. – the Circling practice is unique in that **it prioritizes connection and truth-telling above all else**. It does not specifically *exclude* ideas, plans and stories; it only requests that, when we share stories and ideas, we filter that sharing from the perspective: am I serving connection here?

And the second distinction which can be helpful, is this: **Circling exposes the meta-conversation** – the thoughts and emotions that all of us have in ordinary human interactions, but which we rarely speak, or speak fully. This is what makes the practice so powerful: because once the in-the-moment emotional truths are being voiced and heard, it becomes possible to take the conversation to a new level, often a level of deep pleasure in which everyone's needs are met, even when they initially seemed diverging. We have all experienced an event such as this. People of a more religious orientation may view this type of event as a miracle, a gift of Spirit. People of a more integral or agnostic mindset might call this "an alethea moment". But regardless of our beliefs, it tends to be a very joyful event.

Circling can be viewed as a relational art form of living from a place where "miracles" happen more frequently.

Logistics of Circling

When circlers first convene in a group, either in person or via webconference, they are often too numerous for a single circle. In this case they form **breakout groups** of the "optimal" size, which is 3 to 9 people. Circling also works well in pairs and it can be done informally (see the later description of **Guerrilla circling**)

There are two common types of circles: **Birthday circles**, in which one individual is the primary focus of attention for the entire group (although with the inclusion of **reveals** and **impacts** from other participants), and **Organic circles**, in which the attention flows back and forth between all participants. Depending on the particular "flavor" of Circling (see below), there will be one or two designated leaders, and a fee which is usually quite modest. There is also a variation of an organic circle called a **Surrendered Leadership circle**, in which the leaders are willing to "surrender" any particular group structure, either totally or partially, in response to what they perceive as the group need. This is further described in the Advanced Practices chapter. To note however that "surrender", sometimes known as "welcome everything" is integral to the practice in all schools of Circling.

Additional logistical details, which are important to know when running circles, are covered in Bryan Bayer's book. Since this book is intended as an introduction to the participant role, and since I am taking you on a dive which (I am hoping) will be deeper than it will be comprehensive, I will refer readers interested in leading circles to Bryan's book. It is important to say, however, that everyone in a circle is a leader, and indeed that is at the very core of the power and magic of the modality, that **in a circle one can lead from any position** (and thus the collaborative power of the group is multiplied). I will return later to this topic of what "leadership" actually means in a circle.

Why Circle?

What are the benefits of Circling, why engage the practice? There are several entry points into the practice, all of which play off each other.

1. Circling is fun!

The experience of being seen and accepted for who we really are, and the sense that we are connected to other human beings and part of a larger whole, is one of the most satisfying of all human experiences. Almost everybody knows how pleasurable this experience can be, and yet most of us move along this path of connecting deeply with others in a haphazard way, achieving success only by accident, as it were.

Unlike most "ordinary" human interactions, such as the kind of conversations that happen in bars, around the water-fountain at work, at church, or even in our families, Circling carries an explicit intent to deeper connection. We go into Circling with the shared desire to "know and be known" in all our humanity, whether our inner experience be glorious or unbearably painful.

Through this agreement to join with others, for a pre-set time, in a shared purpose that includes revealing our truth, Circling tends to cut through the bullshit and the games that we all play, and move us fast into a deeper level of sharing.

2. Circling is developmental

Ultimately, circling is a training in human relationships and in self-love. Self-love, self-acceptance and the quality of our human connections are perhaps the most important predictors of happiness, while gaining skill in human relationships is probably the most impactful thing we can do to become more effective in both our personal life and in business. Circling helps us to expand our inner and outer worlds, increase our wisdom and discernment, and become happier, more loving and more effective human beings.

An alternative way of saying this, is that **Circling helps us to uncover our relational blind spots**. We all have patterns, ways of being, unhealed hurts and wounds that may push people away and block an experience of deeper intimacy, or deeper friendship and collaboration. When we get immediate feedback from people about how we occur to them, and especially when that feedback is coming from a place of their wanting to connect with us and get our world, those wounded places become sharper and more clearly defined. From there, our "hurt zones" tend to soften and change into something beautiful, something holy. After being seen in this way, we are often shocked and amazed that we did not get this earlier, realizing that the real situation, the emotional truths and unconscious beliefs underlying our behavior, were obvious to everyone except ourselves. This is the gift of relatedness, of being able to "see ourselves through the eyes of others". What's more, by letting people into our lives and by allowing them to impact us in a positive way, even when they tell us things that might be initially painful, we often help to heal them too.

3. Circling is a global movement for creating a better society

Let me quote Bryan Bayer on this:

> *"Imagine a world in which individuals, cultures and nations related with each other by tapping into this capacity for mature empathy, deep connection, and authentic relating. The relating skills cultivated through the practice of Circling result in a less fear-based and dualistic world, and more of a connection-based, integrated world. This is more of the world that I want to live in, for myself and my children".*

I believe, along with Bryan and many others, that Circling is a truly revolutionary practice which, if it were more widely understood, would change human culture and alter the course of human history. By uniting the personal and the political, Circling sits at the leading edge of human evolution and human transformational technologies – perhaps even more so than any other human transformational modality. Not to mention the fact that it's very affordable!

History of Circling

It seems that the practice we now call "Circling" emerged and was discovered independently by at least 3 different groups, starting as early as 1995. Its precise origins are unknown. It does seem, however, that the first paid groups, and the first use of the "Circling" name, began in the year 1998 in the Bay Area. It was called the Arete Experience and was an intense all-immersive weekend which was led by Guy Sengstock and Jerry Candelaria.

Guy Sengstock was an artist, philosopher, personal trainer, bodybuilder and a massage therapist, while Jerry was at the time working to become a Landmark Forum leader. They had a powerful experience together at Burning Man, with a group that had moved from conflict into a kind of collective ecstasy, and had committed together to take the practice into the world. Besides the influence of Burning Man and Landmark Education, the early practice of Circling was inspired by modalities that include Gestalt, Rave culture and drugs, Carl Rogers encounter groups, man/woman ideas originating from Lafayette Morehouse, the Sterling Men's course, David Deida, Holotropic breathwork, Ali Hameed Almaas's Diamond Heart, the philosophy of Martin Heidegger, and more. The Arete Experience ran until 2009, when it shut down.

Even before this, Bryan Bayer and Decker Cunov had independently discovered the practice as a tool to resolve conflicts in their shared college household in Missouri, later moving to San Francisco and expanding the practice into a community called Soul 2 Soul, which later grew into Authentic SF, one of the first "Authentic" communities which has now spread to over 60 cities. Bryan and Decker found Guy and Jerry in about 2003 and trained with them, later developing the Integral style of Circling, with the help of others at Boulder Integral. Bryan Bayer calls those early years the "Wild West" days of Circling – anything would go.

In 2004, Bryan and Decker founded the Authentic Man Program (AMP) which is an application of Circling into sexual and romantic partnership, and which gained worldwide influence through their DVD training series. AMP is still running in Boulder. Around this time, Alexis Shepperd and Shana James, who were directly involved in the first AMP's as well, developed a parallel program for women which is called the Authentic Woman Experience (AWE), and which continues to be offered in the Bay Area. Alexis Shepperd and Guy Sengstock started leading Arete together approximately 2005. Powerful community, friendships and collaborations emerged out of all these ventures (Arete, Authentic SF, AMP and AWE).

When Arete shut-down in 2009, Bryan and Decker inherited the Bay-area community, and Guy went quiet for a while. When he rejoined the scene, Guy and Alexis Shepperd designed a training program called the Transformational Coach Leadership Training (TCLT). Decker had met Robert MacNaughton, who had been working with Ken Wilber at the first Integral Center in Boulder. Robert went to a TCLT weekend with Guy in the Bay Area, and came home transformed and inspired. He started offering Circling in his living room once a week. Over several years the events became so popular that the crowd of 30+people overwhelmed the space. Robert and Decker started renting space at the Integral Center in the hope of expanding the practice.

In 2011, the first Integral Center (which was created under the direction of Ken Wilber and later taken over by Jeff Saltzman) was about to shut-down. Robert and Decker decided, with great trepidation, to lease the property and take over the business, ultimately building a large Circling community in Boulder, which includes their T3 Training program. They also co-created the Aletheia weekend, which in many ways follows the original Arete model of a three-day weekend of breathwork, Circling, and community processing. In the meantime, Guy Sengstock and Alexis Shepperd created the Circling Institute in the Bay Area, which now runs weekends and year-long training programs, in parallel with the activities of Boulder Integral. Circling and Authentic Relating Games communities started blossoming everywhere, notably in Austin, Texas.

The Austin community was founded by Sara Ness, Jordan Allen, and others. Sara had been a college student, had discovered Authentic Relating Games, had introduced them into her college dorm with great success, and has since, working 70 hour weeks, trained hundreds of facilitators and created dozens of communities through her Authentic Leadership Facilitation Training (ALFT), in addition to the large community in Austin.

In the meantime, two young men from the UK who were interested in Integral theory and ran a Tennis academy, Sean Wilkinson and John Thompson, had also independently discovered the practice in 2002. They started practicing on each other 24 hours a day. In 2008 they found Decker Cunov and trained with him and later with Guy Sengstock, ultimately founding Circling Europe in 2012, which is based in the Netherlands.

The online Circling platform CircleAnywhere.com, which is a product of Circling Europe, launched in 2015 and now serves people from all over the world who are not able to meet in person, or who live far from a Circling center. Authentic World, a product of Boulder Integral, also offers online circling, authentic relating games and a think-tank of best practices and trends. Three other circling schools opened, two of them this year: Amy Silverman's Connection Movement (2013), Josh Stein's Circling Wizardry (2017), and Jason Digges and Ryel Kestano's ART International (also 2017).

The Circling movement, and its twin brother which is Authentic Relating Games, are, as of now (2017), less than 20 years old. And yet there are already over 60 communities worldwide, mostly in the US and in North-Western Europe, and 6 schools offering advanced training. Review the Resources section of this guide for details.

Thus, it could be argued that the "Wild West" stage of Circling is far from over; rather it is just beginning! I personally look forward with great excitement and anticipation to further expansion and development of the practice, which seems to be inevitable.

More information on the history of Circling can be found in Adam Coutts' epic post here:

http://www.intromeditation.com/Wordpress/a-history-of-circling/

More information about the Circling Europe lineage here:

http://circlingeurope.com/what-is-circling/the-lineage-of-circling/

And this article by Sara Ness speaks to the tension between the two founders of Circling, along with some personal stories:

https://www.authrev.com/2015/07/17/my-authenticity-isnt-real/

Refer also to Chapters 2, 4 and 5 in which I attempt to put Circling into the larger context of the "we-space movement" and mention other models and paradigms that are very compatible and which seek to achieve the same goals.

Who owns the "Circling" brand? And what is the relationship of Circling to the Authentic Relating movement?

Not everyone agrees on what "Circling" really is, and there is still some controversy in terms of what some people do under the "Circling" brand. Circling is an open-source brand, and therefore anybody can, theoretically, offer a program and call it "Circling". **I define Circling as any practice of un-withheld, present-moment connection to self and others**, particularly when it involves an agreement around "welcome everything", aka "surrender"** (and thus is quite similar to encounter-group or T-group, with the exception that in Circling, "stories" are permissible to the extent that stories are actually happening inside all of us in the present moment; and also all Circling carries an explicit focus on "getting each other's worlds". Without that, if the group is only for self-expression or emotional discharge, it's not Circling). I personally have not yet seen anything offered under the Circling brand that does not meet my definition of Circling, or that I would not recommend. Of course all the offers are different and there are differences in quality and price-point, as you would expect. In the Resources section of this guide I include comments differentiating the three "major lineage" schools of Circling.

There is also a question of whether the practice of Authentic Relating Games is in the Circling lineage, or is a different modality. My take on that question, is that the Authentic Relating movement includes three practices: Circling, Authentic Relating games, and **Guerrilla Circling**, which is Circling people invisibly (i.e. without explicit context or agreement), and is described in this book. I invented the name "Guerrilla circling", but the practice has been around since the very origins of Circling. I would passionately argue that the reason that Circling is so powerful, the reason for its early success in San Francisco and for its very rapid expansion, is precisely this, that you can make it into a 24×7 practice with the people in your environment, whether they are aware of your intentions or not. I go more deeply into this distinction in chapter 2.

Organization of this book

This book is organized as follows:

1. **Chapter 1** (this chapter) gives you the "30,000 foot view" of the modality and describes the benefits
2. **Chapter 2: Circling Basics** is a deeper dive into circling as a presence practice, and introduces the key distinction of *Guerrilla Circling*.
3. **Chapter 3: Best practices** is an introduction to how we actually Circle, and to dealing with some of the challenges that are likely to arise
4. **Chapter 4: Circling Perspectives and Advanced Practices**, and **Chapter 5: Complementary Modalities** list additional models and communities that can widen your perspective and deepen your practice.
5. The **What Next**, **Resources** and **Leader Formats** chapters will help you find a group, or even start your own groups, either in-person or online.
6. The **Stories** chapter tells some participant stories (so far only mine).
7. **Tips for Giving and Receiving Negative Feedback** is a primer on using *Ownership Language*

Happy reading, and good luck with your practice!

CHAPTER 2: CIRCLING BASIC CONCEPTS

"There is no place to get to but more here" – Decker Cunov, co-founder of Circling

What is Circling, really?

Circling has been described as "equal parts art form, meditation, and group conversation". But the truth of the matter is that no one has yet come up with a definition that is fully satisfactory or that everyone can agree on. Even among the 3 "major lineage" schools of Circling, there is controversy about whether what some of them are doing accurately represents the "original" form of Circling, as it was created by Guy Sengstock and Jerry Candelaria. This controversy is particularly alive with regards to the Surrendered Leadership (Circling Europe) school.

One of the reason for the difficulty of accurately framing or contextualizing the practice, is that Circling is multi-dimensional and so any attempt to define it will by necessity be limiting. For instance: in the next chapter I will present a relationship and communication model that I am calling "Circling". This model is based on what has worked for me after about 800 hours of Circling practice and successful leadership. Most circlers will agree that what I am presenting here covers some important dimensions of Circling. But Circling is, at most, 30-50% a relationship model. It would be much more accurate to call Circling a presence practice, sometimes known as "we-space", "unified field", or Transpersonal consciousness.

It is impossible to convey the felt-experience of "we-space" in a book. It is an experience which is informally described by circlers as "dropping", as in dropping into connection. It is a kind of softening of boundaries, of surrendering into a larger whole, a sense of completion or of perfection of the present moment. It is a non-verbal experience and as such it can happen without any words being spoken. It is an experience that is quite "contagious": once a critical mass of people in a group "drops" it is quite probable that everyone will feel it. It can be a very pleasurable and calming experience, but it can also be painful, poignant, sad, bitter-sweet. It cannot be created through an act of will, or even the best communication. But when it happens is tends to be very transformational.

As such, do not imagine that you can learn to Circle effectively from a book. Your best bet is to practice with experienced circlers, either in person or on the online platforms. From there, you will exponentially magnify your growth by starting to lead your own groups and/or practicing informally with your loved ones or business associates. The latter modality (practicing "circling" informally with your friends) I am calling **Guerrilla circling** and is covered immediately below.

Formal Circling vs. "Guerrilla Circling"

There is an important distinction to be made between the formal practice of circling and "Guerrilla circling". In the formal practice, there is an assumption ("shared context") of "welcome everything", that people will be interested, or at minimum attempt to respond non-reactively, to whatever shows up. Outside of a formal circle, however, you cannot assume that if you show up in anger, blame, or deep pain, that people will attempt to be receptive to you.

It is a natural human reaction to push away strong emotion of any kind, especially negative or blameful thoughts and emotions, and to respond with judgment and distancing. As a result, many of us walk around with a lot of anxiety, loneliness and pain that has nowhere to go and which then feeds on itself, creating an even greater feeling of separation from other human beings. Hardly anyone, really, gets the quality of attention that would enable them to shift the painful sense of separation that we all feel sometimes, and that some of us feel all the time. Our interactions with people tend to be quite functional, sometimes even the people closest to us. We tend to put a lot of effort into deeply cloaking our humanity. We are taught that this is the way things are and that we just have to get used to it, and we do our best to put a happy face on it (because we fear that if we didn't, we would be even more isolated).

And our effort to pretend that everything is okay when it really isn't, obviously compounds the problem.

But there is good news here, which is that we don't have to cloak our humanity. We can strive for all of our interactions with people to have truth and care in them, which also, ironically, makes us much more effective in all spheres of life. This is the practice of "Guerrilla circling", which I am also covering in this book.

The idea of "Guerrilla circling" is to respond to people from an assumption that everyone desires, at some level, to love and be loved, to know and be known, to *belong*. The need to belong is deeply embedded in the context of being human, for the obvious reason that in the tribal culture from which we came, belonging is life-and-death. The need to belong continues to underlie much of our behavior, but is rarely something that people talk about or even admit. The practice of Guerrilla circling is to interact with people with the assumption that they want to belong, to be valued and cared of, and to be acknowledged for their contributions. It is a fairly simple and extraordinarily powerful practice that consists, fundamentally, in leading with vulnerability, which is further described below, and providing quality attention and compassion to people. It is an exercise that can be done with no prior agreement and which is virtually guaranteed to transform all of your relationships.

CHAPTER 3: CIRCLING BEST PRACTICES

> *"Most people do not listen with the intent to understand; they listen with the intent to reply"* – Stephen Covey

> *"You will always outlive my concept of you. And, I will always have a concept for you to outlive."* – Guy Sengstock, co-founder of Circling

In this chapter we get right into the attitudes and communications that are most likely to serve truth and connection. These are guidelines only and must be tested against your intuition at all times. As such, there are suggestions here that may be wrong or not fit for you. If so, ignore the suggestion. Also, don't try too hard to be a "good circler", just do your best to follow and align with the energy of the group, stay true to yourself, and remember that there is no right or wrong way to do this, and that even the best and most experienced leaders sometimes make "mistakes".

Notes on "Guerrilla Circling"

Since formal Circling and Guerrilla Circling are quite different practices (although with a great deal of overlap), I have attempted to distinguish between the two practices by high-lighting the differences. In this chapter, I will start each section by teaching the formal circling practice, and point out differences in guerrilla circling at the end of each section.

Notice feelings and body sensations

Until we are connected to our felt experience of life, which includes our experience of being in our body in this moment, we have little to give to others in an emotional way.

When you start Circling, you will likely often hear questions in the nature of: *"what are you feeling right now?"*, or *"what is going on for you right now"*, or *"how did that land"* (when someone gives you feedback, or else a significant "reveal" of where they are at in relationship to you). These questions are all an invitation from others to deepen our experience of what it's like to be us, and then to communicate that. **They are asking us these questions** because they want to feel us more in order to get our world.

People have a greater or lesser skill, or ability, to accurately feel into and discern the true nature of their current emotional experience. Some of us are quite "heady" and have trouble identifying and articulating our felt experience. Others feel so much they have trouble distinguishing their deepest and truest emotions in the midst of all the "noise". Almost all of us have trouble, to a greater or lesser degree, in distinguishing our own true feelings and desires from the projections, needs and demands of others, and/or in articulating those feelings in the midst, perhaps, of our fear and anxiety that we will not be received – or worse, that people will be angry and reject us, even as we attempt to express our deepest truths and most tender secrets.

For those of us of a more intellectual orientation, myself included, a question such as "what are you feeling in your body now" can occur as downright annoying, a distraction. Of course we can choose to express that annoyance in a circle, but generally the best attitude is to assume that when someone is inquiring into our felt experience, and/or giving us feedback that they are not feeling us, or else feeling us a lot but without clarity or discernment of what's most important, that their intervention is coming from a desire to connect with us more deeply. And to appreciate them from that place, given their attempt, no matter how awkward, to get to know us.

Connect with the group – up to a point (follow your aliveness)

Once you start noticing your responses to the circle, and have made your best commitment to "presence" (however you interpret this word, but think *non-attachment, non-reactivity, non-doing*), things can get interesting – possibly even extremely interesting. Specifically: your own desires, attachments and aversions will start to surface and you will have a choice to either look at them or space-out (or numb out). You will be faced with choices of whether to communicate your feelings, and how to do it. All kinds of emotions can come up, from boredom to attraction to rage to vague unnameable discomforts and more.

Ideally your attitude towards these thoughts, feelings and sensations would be to "welcome everything". This is fundamental to circling and we will be returning to this idea throughout this book. For now, I only want to suggest you try this: **connect or align with the group as much as possible, but without betraying yourself. In other words,** *follow your aliveness*.

To "follow your aliveness" means to stay close to your truth in relation to yourself and to other people. It does *not* mean always communicating your truth (this topic also we will return to). It means accepting that how you are and what you feel, is okay. You cannot force connection, even though you may enjoy it and think it's a good thing; and you can't avoid feelings of disconnection, even though these feelings may scare you, make you angry and cause you to judge yourself and others, or feel like a failure.

Sometimes in a circle, maybe even frequently, you will either be feeling nothing, or else you won't know exactly what you are feeling or how to articulate it. There is nothing wrong with that and indeed it is inevitable. Don't beat yourself up for it. You can speak of your flat emotional state, of your confusion or whatever, if you like. Or you can just be silent and wait. It's up to you and it's all good.

The closer you stay to your aliveness, and to your truth in relation to other people, the more likely it is that you and the group will "drop" into connection. Learn to trust yourself in that, to trust that your showing up authentically in your fear, confusion, rage, vulnerability or whatever, is not just serving you, but is also serving the group.

The more you circle, formally or informally, the more you will develop this fundamental skill of trusting yourself and your reactions, also known as "trusting your experience". Note that "trusting your experience" may at times involve taking challenges or negative feedback from group members around your true intent and way of showing up, which will carry the "trust" one step deeper, of course. Be aware, as well, that learning to trust yourself and to distinguish and articulate your feelings in an accurate and yet compassionate way, is an "infinite game", something you will likely be working on for the rest of your life. Have some compassion towards yourself, because sometimes it will be hard.

Get Their World: Lead from Attention, Curiosity, and Empathy

To "lead" in a circle means, essentially, **to model to others what we want to happen in the group**. This is much more effective, in Circling and in all human relationships, than demanding to be treated a certain way, or asking other people to be more or less of how they are currently being (although there can be room for that, as well, especially when they feel accepted and seen by us).

Ultimately, everyone wants to be seen, understood, and accepted for their unique qualities and gifts. The more we do this, the more likely it is that other people will reciprocate. But even if they don't reciprocate, the act of offering other people our attention, curiosity, and empathy can be very rewarding.

Curiosity is a desire to know someone, and is the first step of **empathy, the attempt to accurately mirror back to someone their felt experience.**

Genuine curiosity and empathy are extraordinarily effective in human relationships, simply because this is not usually something that people get a lot of. Curiosity about people and the desire to know and be known are universal human longings; and yet almost all of us are, to a greater or lesser degree, wounded or shut-down in this area. Many of us are quite timid in expressing our natural human curiosity towards others, often out of social conditioning about respecting other people's privacy – and while this is true in some cases, in other cases, people are very happy to share their intimate feelings with us. With a little prompting, they might even share things that they have never shared with anybody before – even if they have just met you. Such is the strength of the human hunger for authentic connection.

Expressions of Attention, Curiosity, and Empathy

The primary tool of empathy is called **reflection**. Simply repeat what you heard the person say, maybe even in their exact words. For instance, say:

- *What I hear you saying is... Am I getting it right?*

As a caution here, don't do this mechanically. If you are not feeling or understanding what they are saying, you can follow your reflection with a clarifying question:

- *... but I am not sure I am fully getting you (and I want to get you), because I don't understand...*
- Or else: *but I am still a bit confused about...*

For the rest, providing curiosity and empathy is, for the most part, fairly simple. Try any of the following:

- *"What's it like to be here with us (or, to be the center of attention)?"*
- *"How is it to share that with us?"*
- *"I am curious about..."*
- *"You seem upset right now (or angry, or irritated, or anxious, or peaceful, or soft...). Is that true? If so, can you say more about that?*
- *"I am imagining that you feel..."*

Another frequently-used (and very effective) aspect of empathy is called **validation**, the attempt to articulate their felt experience in a way that lets them know that you understand why they are feeling this way and you approve of them as such. You can try:

- *"That makes sense to me because..."*
- *"If I were in your shoes, I would be angry all the time at so-and-so, etc., and so I find it quite amazing that you are able to behave so lovingly"*
- *"Of course you are doing that (or feeling that way), I can totally get it because..."*.

You can improvise endlessly around these themes. It is really quite unusual for people to *not* respond to genuine curiosity, or to attention that is coming from a place of interest and with no ulterior motives, at least motives that you are aware of. In fact, most of the time, it is we who are hung-up about asking sensitive questions, and not the people that we have curiosity about. Even in a situation with a stranger, you can often "prepare" them for a sensitive question by asking permission or expressing vulnerability, as in:

- "*I am shy about asking you this, but...*"
- "*I am intrigued by you and wonder if you would be willing to tell me about...*"
- and you can also open with an appreciation: "*You occur to me as a very open person, so I am going to take the chance to ask you this...*".

Try this. You may be shocked at the results.

Cautions

- In offering empathy you will need to accept that sometimes you will be dead wrong in discerning or articulating another person's feelings. If so, take it gracefully. There is no need to defend yourself or justify what made you think this way about them. Besides, it's highly probable that even if you *are* dead wrong, that your suggesting to someone of how they might feel will help them get clearer. It is also important to use **ownership language** here (see later on). You really cannot know how someone else feels, you can only *take a guess, and then ask them if you are right*.
- You may be deeply curious about an aspect of someone that they don't want to reveal or that makes them very uncomfortable. You have to be sensitive to this. Don't take it personally if they don't want to share, or even if they get angry at the question. The rule of thumb here is: don't restrict your genuine curiosity, and ask the question anyway, up to the point in which it becomes clear that this is a direction that they don't want to go. Honor yourself in asking the question you are curious about, and also honor the other person and respect their right to not answer.

Validate and Appreciate

Besides providing attention, curiosity and empathy, offering validation and appreciation are also practices which are virtually guaranteed to transform all your relationships, in Circling and outside of it. This may seem obvious, but the practice is so powerful and so simple, at least in theory, that it bears repeating.

Most of us resist telling people that we find them interesting and attractive, or their ways of being that we find loveable, courageous or intriguing. We all have our reasons for withholding, and we are also victims of a great deal of cultural conditioning relating to the inappropriateness of communicating feelings, be they positive or negative. But to achieve mastery in human relationships, it is *absolutely essential* to kill, once and for all, our internal messages that telling people how much we like them, or the reasons that we appreciate them, is inappropriate.

Part of the difficulty here is that giving sincere appreciation is, oddly, scary. In addition to cultural conditioning, we may fear that telling people how much we like and admire them will be taken as a disguised attempt to get something from them, or get them to like us in return – and indeed this may be the case, we may need to examine our motives. Furthermore, there are cases where giving positive feedback and appreciation is simply not appropriate: you will probably not want to tell your boss how sexy you find them. At least not in the staff meeting. You have to be sensitive to whether a person *wants* to be appreciated, and the *kinds* of appreciation they may be seeking. This can be tricky.

Nonetheless, the simple truth is that 90% of people will respond positively to a sincere compliment, validation or appreciation 90% of the time. And in many cases, even when they are *not* overly effusive or responsive to the appreciation, or dismiss it entirely (*"you like that dress? That's just an old thing"*), they will secretly enjoy it and feel closer to you. So do not be overly timid.

Guidelines and Cautions

Appreciation and validation have some dangers, which relate mostly to other people's perception of your sincerity and to the quality of your own vulnerability (i.e. it's not a one-way street). Here are some guidelines.

- It is very important to make an effort to appreciate someone for their impact on you, rather than your assessment or judgment about them, no matter how positive. "Praise" (sharing your positive judgment of someone) can be seen as the flip-side of blame, and may be manipulative. For instance: it is better to say *"You seem so courageous to me, and I am so inspired by that"* than *"you are so courageous"*. It is possible that a person might not see themselves as courageous, and if that is true, they will likely be more receptive to your communicating the impact they are having on you, which is inarguable for them, than in accepting that they are indeed, courageous. Your statement will be more believable and more powerful. (Note: this is another instance of the benefit of "trying to make an unarguable statement", as discussed below).
- By the same token, it is best to appreciate something *specific* about them, rather than to make a general statement about them. For instance: *"I love you so much"* is not a bad thing to say, but it might be more effective to say *"I love how clear you are in articulating what is important to you and in asserting your boundaries"*. The latter statement gives more *information*. Sometimes this is referred to as "give a specific frame". A "frame" is a specific event in time *("I felt you the most when you said...")* rather than a general statement.
- In appreciating someone, be careful of "people pleasing". In other words, value whether your appreciation has truth, depth and importance to you, more than you value trying to make the other person happy and relaxed, or to have them like you more. Of course, your desire to please can be present. That is fine but you may want to own it. You could say something like, *"I know this is stupid, and maybe inappropriate, but I wish you could see things how I do, of how harshly you are judging yourself and that your behavior isn't as bad as you imagine it to be"*. What you are owning up to here is your desire to make them happy. It's

not your job to make other people happy, and especially not in circling ☺.
- Be direct and be succinct. Don't go on and on about how wonderful they are. The goal here is to give them something to reflect on, so be brief and put the attention back on them as quickly as possible.
- Finally, consider the idea that the skills of directness and brevity are actually something to practice in all of your human interactions, so start now with the "easy communications", and then once you get better at it, move on to the more difficult communications, in which brevity will be even more important.

Guerrilla Circling: Compliments and Appreciations

Compliments and appreciations are extremely powerful for creating connection, especially when there is not an implicit context for connection such as exists in a formal circle. As such, compliments and appreciations have a big place in Guerrilla circling.

In Guerrilla circling you can be much more relaxed and uninhibited in giving compliments and appreciations. While you would never want to be insincere, it is more permissible in guerrilla circling to give compliments out of a pure desire (or at least part-desire) to have an impact on somebody and to have them notice you, like you and want to be your friend. This takes us into some grey zones of human relationship (is it okay to manipulate someone for their own good?). It is a deep question, but there is a rule-of-thumb which you might find helpful. Ask yourself: **do I have a sincere desire to contribute to another person by communicating something true about myself and how I perceive them? And (important) is this communication likely to be a contribution to them?** If you don't get a clear "yes" to those two questions, maybe it's best to remain silent. As an alternative to expressing direct appreciation, you can communicate interest, attraction or connection intent to someone non-verbally; and you can also visualize connection (check the Heart Math process, www.HeartMath.com – this is actually very powerful).

But with those caveats: don't hold back. Try and imagine what the person would like to hear, and if it is at all true for you, just say it. Sometimes it is even okay to communicate sexual interest or attraction towards strangers (in a formal circle it is virtually always okay to communicate attraction). But use your judgment and don't take it personally if the person rejects your appreciation.

Lead from Vulnerability

In addition to offering curiosity, empathy, and appreciation, which are aspects of trying to elicit and understand another person's felt experience, you will also want to reveal your own felt experience. Sharing your true feelings, and especially those feelings which you are most afraid to reveal, angry, ashamed, or guilty about (the "unacceptable" feelings), is the second key aspect of leadership in Circling.

Why is sharing vulnerability such a powerful practice for creating connection? **First because it is a courageous act of love**. **People usually want to know us**, they want to feel connected to us and get our world. When we share our feelings with people without a demand or expectation that they respond in any particular way, we give other people the opportunity to contribute to us. The difference between "complaining" and vulnerability is that in true vulnerable sharing we are opening ourselves up to feedback, rather than speaking for the pleasure of hearing our own voice or of making ourselves look better than other people. True vulnerability opens up a dialogue, and for this reason it tends to be very attractive; but it's also taking a risk, because people may not be interested in contributing to us in that moment, and because they may respond with fear to our vulnerability or be repelled by it. Vulnerability can be scary, on both the sending and the receiving end of it, and this is perhaps what makes it so interesting and exciting. Nonetheless, in many cases people will thank us afterwards for telling them how we really feel, for opening up a conversation that has the potential for being transformational for everyone.

And the second reason why sharing vulnerability creates connection, is that **often people see it as permission to share more of themselves as well**. Typically, as we share more, so do they, which then gives us permission to say even more and get more real still. Ideally, this keeps on amplifying so long as we are with the person, or with the group; and the next time we come back together, we continue where we left off and maybe go deeper still.

You may find this experience quite addictive. You may find that you can't get enough of it. Some people, including myself, believe that humans are meant to relate like this all the time. But we tend to forget about the power and importance of curiosity, empathy and vulnerability. We tend to forget the extraordinary impact that these simple practices can have on others and ourselves.

Most of us have a great deal of attention on ourselves, on our own thoughts, problems and needs. Learning to enlarge that circle of attention is the essence of becoming more fully human. We do this by paying attention to others – deep attention – and then reflecting back to them what we see, or imagine, of their internal state. Almost everyone will brighten visibly when you do this with them.   It is even possible that it will be the first time in their lives that they receive real kindness from anyone, or that they feel entirely seen and understood by another human being. It's possible that in one minute, you can alter the course of their life.

Cautions

Being vulnerable means to share both positive and "negative" feelings that you may have towards yourself and others. **In choosing what to share and what to hold back, you have to judge whether you are serving truth and connection.** This is not always easy to determine.

In Circling, as in all human relationships, you can (and should) be very uninhibited about sharing positive feelings you have towards others. You can also be fairly uninhibited in sharing your own fears, anxieties and inadequacies about yourself. You do, however, need to be cautious in sharing negative feelings towards others. When you do feel a need to share negative feelings, it really ought to come from a place of commitment to connection – of wanting to enter a space of truth with someone with the goal of achieving deeper understanding of them and of yourself, but without a demand for agreement or closure or even listening. It's also very important to use "ownership language", which I will talk about next.

Thus it is quite important to examine your own motives prior to sharing negative feelings with another person. To the extent there is any sense of "make-wrong" towards the other person, and that you are speaking to them out of a demand that they change their behavior in order to please you or ease your own suffering, or out of a desire to teach them something such as the "correct" way to behave, you need to go back to the drawing board and find a different attitude or style of expression. This is especially true when you feel a sense of rightness, or even "righteous indignation" about their behavior. If you don't do this, the other person might hear you say (and this may in fact be true), that their way of being is distressing to you, that you judge them for it and you want them to immediately stop – as opposed to your communicating your judgments of them, or anger or upset, out of a sincere desire to understand why they are being this way, so that you can (hopefully) make peace with it and return to a space of mutual caring and understanding.

In addition to the above, the fact of your having a strong reaction to someone in the nature of "righteous indignation", along with a reduced sense of empathy towards them, points directly and irrefutably to something powerful that has been triggered in you and which you are trying to fix in them. This could be a good time to share and reflect on what's going on for you, rather than attempting to fix them.

In a formal circling context with a skilled facilitator, if you're not sure whether you're triggered or not, or what your motive is for sharing a negative feeling, my advice would be: try sharing it anyway, and trust in the ability of the group to help you figure out what is happening. As a powerful way to invite inquiry into your experience, you can state something along the lines of *"I'm not sure what my motive is in sharing this, but it feels important"*. This is a great way to turn a confusing impulse into vulnerable leadership: *"I feel this and I want to share it but I don't know why or even whether I should share it."*

Guerrilla Circling, Negative feedback, and an NVC Primer

When practicing Guerrilla Circling, such as in every-day conflict situations with people in your life, you have to be even more careful, more discerning and more disciplined about giving negative feedback.

The reason for that has already been stated: you can't assume a person in your life who hasn't circled, such as a house-mate or business associate, is going to have skill and commitment to explore the space of connection with you. It is possible that they are angry and blameful towards you and have little interest in investigating the connection space between the two of you, which may be non-existent from their perspective. It's possible they just want you to change or adapt to them in order to ease their own suffering, and they may not be very receptive to your telling them that it's not your job to ease their suffering, and that they need to take greater ownership of their feelings and communicate more responsibly if they want to be heard by you – even though all this may be "true".

The Non-Violent Communication (NVC) model can be extremely helpful in cases such as this. There is a considerable overlap between Circling and NVC, with the difference that NVC does not assume or ask the other person for a commitment to connection. NVC simply assumes that the other person has "needs" – for understanding, affection, belonging, acknowledgement etc. – and then tailoring your attitude and language towards meeting those needs in them (which, hopefully, will calm them down and make them more receptive to you). As such, NVC might be more attuned to the Guerrilla Circling practice.

Let me give an example. Your housemate has been leaving dirty dishes and you feel a sense of outrage. After some introspection you track it down to this belief: "C*aring and responsible people don't leave dirty dishes. My housemate is demonstrating that he is irresponsible and doesn't care for me*". Before you approach your housemate, you would be wise to consider: Is this belief really true?

Have you yourself ever left dirty dishes for your mother to clean up? Are you justifying your anger towards your housemate by imagining that you are right, that there is a right way to behave, and that you have something to teach them about what's right? What are the feelings and needs that might be alive in your housemate? Is it possible they are just overwhelmed and unhappy with their life, and doing their own dishes is difficult for them and has really nothing to do with you? This is the kind of self-inquiry that we ought to consider prior to engaging another person in negative feedback. **Even in cases where you feel completely justified and are dealing with a minimum acceptable behavior that you need to be respected, you would still be wise to approach the other person with curiosity about them, and try to express care rather than your unspoken (covert) or even overt make-wrongs – if you want to be heard, that is.**

Sharing negative feelings with other people can be difficult under the best of circumstances. A "pure" Circling approach would to share vulnerability, admit that you are upset and that you may not even know why: *"As I hear you speak and express your anger, I feel strong resistance to you and also feel totally unseen and disconnected from you, and it is very painful for me"*. But this is probably not a formula that you would want to try with your non-circler housemate who is attacking you for failing to do the dishes. In general, it is always tricky to challenge someone to some way of being that is different than how they are currently showing up (maybe fuller or more true, or more loving, at least from your perspective). This is a complex topic. We will return to it in the "Communicate Responsibly" section.

Share Impact, Offer Reflection and Inquiry

"Sharing impact" is another aspect of vulnerability. It means to let people know how they occur to you, and particularly any emotional reactions you may be having to them: joy, excitement, sadness, anxiety, tension in your body, irritation, boredom, confusion, or whatever. You will particularly want to share any strong emotions that you are having in response to them.

Sharing impact is fundamental to the process of connection. **Most people want to know and are intensely curious about how they occur to others**, but are often afraid of asking directly. Many people, and all of us at times, carry an ongoing internal conversation when we are relating to someone. It might go like this: *is this person liking me? Am I being appropriate here? Do they think I am smart, attractive, lovable...? Do I have bad breath? Are they noticing I forgot to brush my hair, or the stain on my shirt? Etc., etc.* The beauty and power of Circling, as opposed to traditional ways of relating, is that in Circling we seek to expose this "meta-conversation", and we have agreement and permission to do so.

"Impact" can be anything at all that you are thinking and feeling with respect to another person, but also anything that you are imagining that they are thinking and feeling. Technically speaking, what you yourself are thinking and feeling in relation to someone, and what you imagine they are thinking and feeling, are quite different things. But in practice, the two types of sharing will occur together.

Danger zones of sharing impact and offering reflection

- It is a truism that your thoughts and feelings towards another person – let alone your imagining of what they are thinking and feeling – will be colored by your own experiences, fears and projections (and in case you are not already aware of this, Circling will cause you to learn this quite rapidly ☺). These imaginings, or even felt sensations, may not necessarily have any "truth" or reality to the other person, meaning that your reaction may be completely about you. This is in the nature of human relationships, that we are so frequently wrapped up in ourselves and our own experience that we do not see people accurately, and our internal reactions to others are often out of proportion to their real condition and intent. Therefore, you would be wise to be very humble in offering your feelings and perspectives to another person (maybe not all the time – there may be times that being very blunt is called for). But regardless,

always attempt to use "ownership language" and also don't take it personally if the person is unmoved by your impact, or even responds negatively.
- It's also possible that you may be entirely "right" in your analysis or diagnosis of somebody, or in your perception of their deeper emotions, but they won't be ready to hear it or interested in what you have to share. **To share a reflection with someone who is not interested in what you have to say, particularly a negative reflection, is not love, it is violence.** This is not true in 100% of situations (your child may not be interested in your feelings about them playing in the street, but you will still communicate that). But you can generally treat this as an inviolable rule in relating to adults, although note here the important distinction between sharing a "reflection" as a judgment, versus a true vulnerable share that is not making anybody wrong. Your best bet in this kind of situation is either to say nothing at all until you get more internal clarity, or else return to vulnerable sharing, perhaps around your feeling of disconnection from this person. Also refer to the earlier section on "Guerrilla circling and negative feedback" for ideas here.
- You can directly share that you have a judgment, provided that you state upfront that your judgment may not have any reality and that you present it from a desire for clarification rather than it being a truth of any kind.
- With those caveats, however, do not be timid, and particularly if you have a strong reaction to someone, either positive or negative. In general you can assume, until proven otherwise, that a person who is showing up in a circling group is going to be interested and curious about how they occur to people; more so, for instance, than a casual acquaintance might be. It's okay to take risks in your communication.
- By the same token, if you are on the receiving end of a thought or feeling that doesn't fit for you, you can say so, or you can just let it go, knowing that when all is said and done, most anything anybody shares with you is going to be about

them. Remember that by sharing yourself vulnerably, you are not only taking an opportunity to discover yourself at a deeper level, you are giving others an opportunity to discover themselves through you.

Below are some alternative formulations for skillfully sharing negative feelings with people. Note that sometimes it is quite okay to be blunt, and the power of Circling is precisely that, that it's okay to share your truth without worrying too much how the other person will respond. However, there is a thin line between "truth" and violence, as already mentioned. Use discernment, as in the following examples.

Rather than...	Try...
"I am not feeling you"	If you don't feel related to somebody in the circle, the most powerful approach is to try and figure out why. Because a statement such as "I am not feeling you" carries an undertone of *"I should be feeling you and if I am not, it's your fault"*. Think instead: does this person remind you of somebody in your life you have issues with? Are you just having a bad day and struggling to put real attention on anyone? What's it like to want to feel connected to someone, and not be able to? Even if the person is not "relateable" by you, the thoughts and feeling that arise in you from this experience might prove valuable. See the later section "Welcome everything" for more ideas here.
"I feel bored hearing you talk about your mother"	Same as above: explore what it would take to deepen your experience with the other person, and/or look at your own stuff that might be coming in the way. Put some "skin in the game" (your own skin) rather than standing in judgment or indifference to the. You could try:

	"How are you feeling about your mother right now as you are talking?" [provide genuine curiosity, bring it to the present moment]
	Or: *"I would like to understand what is most important for you here. Is this really what you want to talk about? What are you getting from this conversation?* [gently and respectfully challenge, as well as open an inquiry]
	Or: *"I can't explain it, but I have a sense that there is something you want from this conversation that you are not getting. Is this true?"* [Offer an inquiry, but respectfully. Because if the circlee responds "Yes this conversation is exactly what I am needing", then you can back-off your judgment that you, and maybe everyone else as well, is bored, knowing that your attention is actually being received and appreciated. You might then become more engaged]
"Why are you so upset? It happens to everybody"	Rather than expressing a judgment or lack of resonance with somebody upfront, try and look for places of resonance, as in *"I felt you the most when you said…"*. You can always return to negative feedback later, if necessary, and this will certainly be way more impactful once the circlee feels connected to you and senses that you get their world and are on their side

Offering Reflection / Inquiry

To "offer reflection and inquiry" is to ask a question that deepens a person's process, an offer to further distinguish or articulate their felt experience; or, alternatively, to offer them something that occurs to you in your experience of them, in the hope that it will be meaningful or illuminating to them.

Offering useful reflection and inquiry to people is a core skill of circling and a quite advanced one, which can only be learned through practice. This is a complex topic and one of the reasons that people go to advanced circling trainings. Some of it may just consist of "walking through" a person's thinking and feeling experience with them (what they have already shared) and then asking for clarification. It may also involve noticing dissonance between the circlee's words and their non-verbals, and/or articulating feelings that arise in you which seem out-of-sync or unrelated to the circlee's words. I will give just a few examples here, and encourage the reader to pursue some of the resources listed later. (Some of these examples are drawn from Sara Ness's <u>The Art of Getting Somebody's World</u>)

- *"You have used those words, 'I don't feel that anyone cares', three times in this circle. What does that mean for you?"* [Reflect and inquire]
- *"You seem to be feeling something intense right now. I feel drawn to this. Are you willing to stay there with us?"* [Reflect, empathize, appreciate, offer to slow it down]
- *"What are you thinking about as you are looking around?"* [Bring it to the present moment]
- *"When you say 'I don't know', what is going through your mind (or, how does that feel in your body)"?* [Curious and inquire]
- *"I've always thought you were scared of me. Is that true?"* [Vulnerable share and curiosity]
- *"When I ask how you are feeling, you seem angry, and I imagine you don't want to be asked. Is that true?"* [Reflect, empathize, inquire]
- *"Did anyone else in the room think that he was angry?"* [Engage the room, seek other perspectives]
- *"You say you feel sad right now, but I notice you smiled after you said that. Did you notice that? What were you thinking?"* [Reflect dissonance and inquire]

- When you hear a long explanation: *"Are you afraid that we are not going to understand you?"* [Reflect, inquire]
- When the group is asking a lot of question, and the circlee gives short responses: *"It seems that we really want to get to know you. Do you want to be known by us?"* [Reflect, gently challenge]
- *"We have touched three times on your desire to be accepted by us, but every time you say that you make a joke. Is it uncomfortable or scary for you to reveal that?"* [Reflect dissonance and inquire]
- *"What are you getting from this circle"*, or *"is there something shifting as you are talking?"* [Bring it back to the present moment]

Guerrilla Circling and sharing impact

You have to be more cautious sharing impact in Guerrilla Circling. In essence you have to be more discerning of what the other person is able to (or wants to) hear from you. You need to have (proportionately) more attention on them and less on yourself and your own needs than you would in a formal circle (partly because in a formal circle you will also get help from the facilitators or other participants, while in Guerrilla Circling you will likely be on your own and there is therefore a greater risk that you can mess up really badly). In Guerrilla Circling the connection intent (or listening) may not be so strong, so you want to do your best to make sure that you are really serving truth and connection in the interaction, rather than "talking above them" or asking them to share a context which they may not have a clue about, and which they might think is ridiculous even if you tried to explain it to them. Reverting back to straight-up NVC, as already described, can be quite helpful here.

Own Your Experience (Communicate Responsibly)

"Owning your experience" means to frame your communications more in terms of your feelings, needs and desires in relationship to another person, and less in terms of your beliefs or judgments about the person, the reasons that you think this person is the way they are, or the things they are saying which you think are wrong. This is, once again, a very complex topic which we can only brush on here. You may want to check resources in Non-Violent Communication for ideas (Google Erik Erhardt's paper Can we talk), and also explore a modality called Clean Talk, which is even more rigorous than NVC. Much of these practices involve getting internal clarity about the judgments and beliefs that underlie many of our communications, and then re-stating them from a perspective of our feelings and needs, rather than the unowned or unexpressed judgment.

Returning to the previous example: the judgment *"responsible people do their own dishes"* (or *"kind people do not talk like this"*): even if these judgments are "true", this won't help you change the other person's behavior one iota, if they disagree with you or feel attacked by you, which is probable after hearing something like this. So, rather than coming at the person from this belief that is about your making them wrong for their behavior, you might open with a feeling statement, or even a vulnerable share, such as *"I get really irritated with you when you leave dirty dishes and then I feel disconnected from you"*; and then prepare to give empathy, at least to the extent that you are capable of it in the moment.

Some people call this "responsible communication", and it is, unfortunately, quite rare. The normal, or "default" way that people communicate negative feelings is *virtually guaranteed* to increase reactivity on both sides and create distance. This style of communication is unlikely to further your goal, whether it be to get closer to another person, or else to get them to do something that you want, such as listen to you or provide empathy. You may feel momentarily better about "giving them a piece of your mind", but in the end you will both likely be unhappy and unfulfilled. You may even get into a cycle of reactivity with someone, of demands and counter-demands, threats and accusations, which can go on for years – when, perhaps, a direct statement of your need and simple acknowledgement of them and their need, would immediately solve the problem. This is the reason we call this type of communication "irresponsible", but it would be just as accurate to call it "stupid communication": nobody is being served by it. At best, you are wasting everybody's time and energy, including your own. Responsible communication is a tough skill to practice when we are angry and upset with someone, or judging them to be bad and wrong. We all struggle with it.

Using ownership language well is an art form, however there is a rule-of-thumb which you might want to attempt: **try and make an unarguable statement – a statement that nobody can disagree with because it references your own feelings, for which you are the undisputed authority**. This will not entirely stop people from challenging you or wanting to argue with you, but it will probably decrease their reactivity and make them more receptive to you. As already noted, owning your experience is especially important when giving someone negative feedback, or sharing about something that they are doing that is distressing to you or that makes you feel more distant from them.

Guerrilla Circling and ownership language

In your everyday life, just as in Circling, you *will* find "difficult people" who challenge you in some way or upset you in their way of being. In communicating your anger or distress with them, you will have to be careful not to lose them completely, to the point they won't want anything to do with you (unless that is also your intention, that you don't want anything to do with them – but in that case why talk to them at all?). In Guerrilla Circling with such people, it will sometimes be necessary to soften your impact, especially if they are also angry or upset, and/or return to empathy until they calm down sufficiently to be able to listen to you. Sometimes you will need to give up telling them everything, all the things they do which are offensive to you, in one sitting.

Nonetheless, consider this idea: that it may be better to say "something" to them rather than to say nothing at all, even if that something is quite gentle, a tiny fraction of your true feelings towards them. If you don't say anything at all, you may well suffer for it afterwards, and therefore to be silent is being unkind towards yourself and unkind towards them (because you will continue to be upset with them, which they truly do not want regardless of the terrible things they may be saying to you). They may really welcome an opportunity to clear the air with you, or they may be totally unaware of the negative impact they are having on you and be grateful to you for letting them know. It is extremely important, however, in such a case to use as full ownership language as you possibly can.

I return to this topic in the two sections below "Make Right, Not Wrong" and "Honor Yourself".

Make Right, Not Wrong (Find People Right, Approve of them)

When you are reacting to someone in a negative way, and judging them wrong for how they are being, it can be helpful to take on the following perspective: people are the way they are for a reason, they are the product of their genes and of the environment that nurtured them (or not); and consequently it is *certain* that if you were born into their body and had the experiences they had, you would behave exactly the same.

This is sometimes referred to as "***finding people right***", and is one of the most important skills that you could ever master, if you hope to be effective as a human change agent. It is actually one of the great paradoxes of human relationships: that **people change a lot faster in the direction that you want (or that they want for themselves), when they are first accepted as they are**.

Approving of other people does not mean that you will always agree with them or feel their behavior is justified. It means that **you will attempt to find <u>something</u> to agree with, empathize or appreciate about them.** This is not always easy, and in some cases you may find it impossible, but usually you will find that even a small effort in that direction will give huge dividends in dealing effectively with difficult people and interactions. At minimum, it should give you more peace of mind with regards to the situation, which holds the potential for increasing your mental clarity and designing an effective intervention, should one be necessary.

The reason that "finding people right" is so effective is that it reflects a fundamental reality of the human condition: that none of us owns the truth, or the whole truth, of what is best for the world, for other people, or even for ourselves. "Truth" in human relationships can only be found by agreement. Another way to say this is that "**in relationship, everyone is right**". Taking that perspective will, in most cases, be a win for everyone, providing a fertile ground from which a positive conversation might emerge. Indeed, one of the reasons that Gandhi, Martin Luther King and other powerful world peace leaders were so effective is that they recognized the *humanity* of their opponents, even as they actively worked to unseat them and their ideas.

"That which we resist, persists" said Werner Erhart. "Resist not evil" said Jesus. Jesus offered that perspective even in matters where we might be certain that evil is present. Imagine how much *more* true that perspective will be, in the vast majority of cases in which we really cannot be certain of what is right and wrong?

Be Impactable

"Being impactable" is an advanced form of empathy and is the essence of what transformative relationship is all about. The idea there is when people share something sensitive about themselves, they are usually not interested so much in your thoughts or judgments about their experience, whether you think they are right or wrong to be feeling and thinking as they are. But they are, usually, *very* interested in your ability to get their experience and to be moved by it. And above anything else, they will likely be *passionately* interested in anything they say which you could apply creatively to yourself, something that could brighten your world or change something in you. It is a universal human longing to want to have an impact on other people.

Let me quote Sara Ness here:

Let yourself be affected by others' experience. Empathize from your own world, remembering similar experiences or feelings in your past. Let yourself be touched by how they are showing up right now with you. Be so here that you could be destroyed by this connection – and over time, you will discover your own invincibility.

Guerrilla Circling and "Being Impactable"

"Being Impactable" is even more effective in Guerrilla Circling, for the simple reason that people probably won't expect it. They may be charmed and thrilled by the fact that you have the courage to tell them how they are affecting you.

For these reasons, you may want to double-up your positive impact statements in real life and with the people in your environment. To fail to communicate emotional impact towards someone when it is present, is both cruel and stupid, because you could make a real difference to someone by doing so, and because you could make a new friend or ally.

Honor Yourself (Handling Conflict)

To "honor yourself" means to take care of yourself emotionally in your interactions with people. Specifically, it means that you do not have to do anything that doesn't feel right to you, answer any question, accept anybody's feedback, or be any particular way, regardless of what anyone says – even a group leader! You even have an option to walk out of a group (or hit the "close" button in an online group) – I have done it once or twice myself, and I have threatened to do it many other times!

Dropping out of a group should be considered a measure of last resort, hopefully to be done only *after* you have expressed your ambivalence about what is happening, or even rage, and haven't felt heard in that; however it is always an option, and you should not judge yourself for leaving a group if you feel you have to do it, or judge anyone else for it either. Indeed in some cases it might be the responsible thing to do: better to leave the group and let yourself cool off, than to explode at them in your rage at how bad and wrong they are, or all the ways in which they are not getting your world or even putting you down.

(Note: leaving a group is controversial. What I am giving you here is my perspective on it, which may or may not be shared by others. It is very important for me personally to have choice which relationships are empowering to me and which ones are not, and not to engage with a group out of a sense of obligation. Of course if you are blowing up and leaving groups consistently, that is not a good thing and will have negative impact on people wanting to circle with you).

In practice, it is quite rare for people to leave a group in the middle. It is much more common for people to say nothing, and then feel mild to intense discomfort or anger for hours or days afterwards, and wish that they had said something. It is quite likely you will find most groups very nurturing and connecting, this is the nature of the practice and the power of coming together with connection intent. Nonetheless, conflicts *will* arise, and they can be very valuable to everyone. In many cases, a major conflict in a person's life, or in a group, can be the cause of a deep shift and growth.

As such, you would be wise to value all conflict that comes up in a group, to practice empathy and all the attitudes and skills already covered. It is likely that you will find these attitudes and skills very valuable in other aspects of your life outside of Circling. And so, what better opportunity than to practice now in Circling, when you can probably count on at least a few people in the group to "have your back" and be making an effort to understand your experience and empathize with you?

Guerrilla Circling and "Honor Yourself"

In Guerrilla circling someone who is attacking you and (seemingly) holding no value to "commitment to connection", it can be very powerful for you to stay in connection with them unilaterally. It can help them be seen in a way that they perhaps thought impossible (hence why they wanted to break the connection).

You can do this either in formal circles or else with strangers. Let me give an anecdote on the latter (from the blog of my friend Lisa Campion). This is black-belt level A/R and you may not be up for it. There is nothing wrong with walking away, either (maybe with a negative impact statement: "*I don't like how you are talking to me and I won't participate in this*", or just "*I am sorry, I can't listen to this, I need to walk away*"). You should not push yourself beyond what you have to give.

But here is Lisa's story:

"The other day, I was in what could have been a parking lot rage incident. I was in the Target parking lot and I left my empty shopping cart near my car rather than take it back to the little corral. Mostly because I broke my foot and it's in a walking cast and my foot was aching already. The cart corral suddenly looked like it was a long way away.

Then a gust of wind came along and blew the cart into a man's very nice car. I watched it go feeling like –uh oh and ….ding.

Instantly he became a very angry dude. He ran over to me and was really yelling, how rude, what the hell was my problem, he was on a roll, all purple in the face. He stopped when he saw my foot in the air cast. I apologized but he kept right on going. I could feel that his anger was about something else and I was just the trigger, it was so obvious. The ding had opened up his anger closet, which was full and it all overflowed.

He was projecting this all over me. Of course it is annoying to have your car dinged by a shopping cart (It didn't even leave a mark, truthfully) but his reaction was epic, it was like an 8 out of 10 when maybe the ding was worthy of a 2.

I got very grounded and opened my heart, just as if he was a client in my office. It was an experiment to see what would happen- so I trotted out my therapy voice and said, "Yeah dude, I am really sorry, I can see how mad you are. Anyone would be angry, I totally get it. My cart totally dinged your beautiful car."

Angry Dude: "Yeah well- You should be more responsible and less of a selfish jerk blah blah…" He was off and running again.

Me: "Yes, you are right. Should have put that back where it was supposed to go. I hate it when people are selfish jerks. That sucks."

Angry Dude looked less angry. He blinked a few times. "Yeah well. Next time you should. But maybe you didn't cuz your foot is broken. I can see how maybe you didn't want to walk all the way over there. I had a really tough day at work. My boss is a selfish jerk."

Me: "Dude, that's rough. I work for myself and sometimes I can be a jerk to myself so I know what it's like having a jerky boss."

Angry Dude was no longer angry. It did take him a second to figure that one out, but he sat down on the edge of my bumper and unloaded the trials and tribulations of his life. He was going through a divorce and missed his kids. His life was in a crappy, terrible place and he was feeling lost. I love these moments when I get a chance to do some parking lot therapy so I just listened. This does happen to me on a pretty regular basis and I actually enjoy connecting and listening to people. After a while I said to him that maybe it was a chance to reconstruct his life and what did he think he needed to do to reconnect with his kids and get support for himself? But mostly I just listened.

Eventually, he stood up and said he was glad I bumped into him. (He had a good sense of humor under all that rage!) We shared a handshake and then even a quick hug."

Welcome Everything

The previous section "Honor yourself" describes the more extreme case of "Welcoming everything", which is accepting that conflict will occasionally arise in a group, and as such it is better to welcome what is already present than to resist it (a strategy which is valuable in all human relationships, incidentally). In most cases, however, your reactions and feelings will be less dramatic than presented earlier: boredom, tensions in your body, mild irritation, slight confusion, or distracting thoughts such as *"what am I doing here"* or *"rats, I forgot to take out the garbage"* or *"this is stupid, I would much rather be painting my nails right now"*. To "welcome everything" means to accept whatever thoughts and feelings are arising in the moment as, perhaps, something valuable, something which carries the potential for insight or an interesting and transformative conversation.

Another way of saying this, is to consider the possibility that everything that is happening inside of you in relation to the group is "an excuse for intimacy": meaning that you are in a process of self-discovery, and other-discovery, in a way that is quite mysterious and that *all* of your feelings, no matter how unrelated they may seem, are contributing to that. Furthermore, you can't really avoid these feelings anyway, so you would be wise to surrender to them (see the final section "Surrender Gracefully"). For instance: you might *imagine* that you would be having more fun painting your nails, or washing dishes; and you may be right; but since you have chosen to spend an hour in a circling group, you may as well get as much out of the experience as you can.

This is the aspect of Circling that has being spoken of as "inter-subjective meditation". In classical meditation, you are noticing thoughts and sensations and your internal reactions of attraction and aversion to these sensations, while attempting to not get over-attached or over-invested one way or the other. Ideally, in classical meditation you are taking the perspective that these thoughts and feelings are merely "interesting" – rather than good, bad, completely stupid or life-changing insights. In other words, you are "taking it all lightly". In Circling, the invitation is to do exactly the same: take it all lightly. Trust that whatever truth or falseness, enlightenment or stupidity, will be revealed to you at the right time. In the meantime, your job is merely to pay attention.

It can be frustrating to have to wait for clarity when things don't make sense right away. But experience shows that events that didn't connect up neatly while you were circling, still seem to have a capacity to teach you the lessons they contained, even days or weeks or months later. All you need in the moment is to trust in your self's ability to record and process things in its own time and pace.

It is particularly important to understand and accept that when you are having a strong reaction to someone, either positive or negative, that ultimately it is all about you. Thus, while you might think that you are reacting to someone because of how they are being, and this may be "true" from an ordinary perspective, it would be equally true to say that you are reacting to someone because of something in you that is resonating with them, either positively or negatively. Taking that perspective will help you see *all* the people in your life as a gift to you, since they are helping you gain self-awareness and discrimination – no matter how stupid and irritating they may seem at times.

Slow Down

We live in a culture which generally values performance and achievement more than it values "being", relatedness, or genuine aliveness and emotional connection. Many of us, including myself, carry this valuing of speed over connection into our Circling groups. We talk fast, process things fast, are driven to make our point, fill the space, communicate our deepest truth and get it all done as quickly as possible – even when, ironically, what is trying to "get done" here is connection and transformation, things which generally don't respond well to time pressure. We may fear that if we miss the opportunity to self-express, right now, those few precious minutes of attention and air-time that we are offered will be wasted.

This fear of slowing down is actually not a rational fear, when our intention is connection and depth. Indeed, often the first thing that needs to happen to deepen a group conversation is simply to *start taking our time*. We can choose to appreciate the unfolding mystery of connection as it's happening, more than our desire to fulfill our communication and "transformation" agenda, no matter how urgent or compelling it might seem to us.

So what does "slowing down" look like? It is generally very simple, such as talking more slowly, or not at all, while noticing body sensations or the quality of our connection to others. We slow down, essentially, in order to feel more. A lot of people have trouble feeling and talking at the same time. The solution in such cases is often to talk less, while still holding attention on the person who is being circled. Silence is not a bad thing.

In a group with a skilled facilitator you will probably, at some point, hear some direction such as: *"pause there for a moment. I want to feel into this"*, or *"pause there, I don't want to miss this moment"*. This can be considered a gift: people are giving us feedback about a moment of truth or authentic connection which we would entirely miss, if we were to continue in the bulldozer action and relentless flow of our thoughts, the ceaseless internal processing that may dominate our life outside of Circling, and perhaps life in the 21st century in general.

To note, however, that having a communication or transformation agenda is *not* in itself a bad thing. Most of us do have some kind of agenda, a need of some kind, no matter how much we are, or pretend to be, all-accepting and open to everything and "spiritual". There is actually a kind of unavoidable tension in Circling, and maybe in all human relationships, between: on the one hand, fulfilling our personal agendas; and on the other hand, being in the moment, in service to others, and "surrendering to 'what is' ". See the later section "The Yin and the Yang of Circling: Connection Intent vs. Developmental Intent" for more about this.

Surrender Gracefully

I conclude this section of best practices with perhaps the greatest and hardest skill of all: the ***art of graceful surrender***.

To "surrender" means, in its best form, one of two things. The personal meaning of "surrender" is to accept the fact that we are a certain way and feel certain things, and to stop fighting with ourselves about that, to stop "the war of sub-personalities". This could also be called "surrendering to the inevitable", in that most of us have little or no control over our feelings (although, ironically, in the act of acceptance of all our feelings, no matter how crazy or "dysfunctional" we imagine them to be, they often transform into something else or recede into the background).

The second aspect of "surrender" is in relation to other people, and it simply means: **Stop trying to change people or argue with them, and accept them as they are. You may even simply decide to do what they want you to do, for their sake, even though it may not be something you need or want for yourself.**

Why would you do this? Because, as the saying goes, *you may decide that it is more important for you to be happy than to be right*. You may make a choice for the higher good.

Graceful (or true) surrender is distinct from "submission" or "appeasement" or even "sacrifice". You are not giving in to demands which you may perceive as selfish and stupid, simply because other people have power over you, or because you want them to shut up and leave you alone. True surrender is *voluntary*. You are offering yourself in service. Graceful surrender is an act of love.

In practice, the difference between graceful surrender and appeasement will take some discernment. You may still be feeling reactive or upset towards the other person; but, ideally, your surrender should give you *some* inner peace and serenity. You will feel a sense of power and self-nurturing in the choice to surrender.

One of the most important acts of surrender that you can do has already been described: it is "finding people right". It is quite ironic that finding people right is actually one of the toughest forms of surrender: ironic because it costs us nothing but our pride, the recognition that other people's truth is just as valid to them, as our truth is to us; and hence our judgment of them as wrong has no reality to it. Often we are more attached to "being right" than we are attached to our money, our health, or even our life.

Conclusion

Practicing these principles will give you a leg-up in all of your human relationships, and also make you a happier person. Formal Circling groups are a (relatively) safe space in which to practice the skills of connection.

And this is why I am so excited to share this with you all! I have found few places outside of Circling where I can meet, to such a degree, the range and depth of those brilliant, loveable, extraordinary, sometimes infuriating but ultimately constantly entertaining creatures: my fellow human beings.

It is true: we do "discover ourselves through the eyes of others".

CHAPTER 4: CIRCLING PERSPECTIVES AND ADVANCED PRACTICES

> *"Trust that people move towards wholeness, and we just have to follow"* – Alexis Shepperd

> *"You don't have to get what you want if you can express what you want"* – Strephon Kaplan-Williams

The previous chapter might be called "Baseline Circling" – shared context or values which most people in circling (maybe not all!) will generally agree with. But there is so much more, both from a practice viewpoint (obviously), *and* a theoretical viewpoint.

This chapter is intended to explore a few of these topics.

Circling, Integral Theory, and the AQAL model

Circling did *not* begin as an outgrowth of Ken Wilber's integral world-view, which includes the AQAL (All Quadrants / All Levels) theory of human development. **However, it is a perfect fit**, and has been embraced by many integral communities, particularly the Boulder Integral Center in which Circling is the leading modality being taught. Circling is actually even better than a "fit" with integral theory, it is a practical and powerful extension of it, a way to live a life more inspired by the integral model, and also a direct response to the criticisms that have been levied on the integral community for being overly intellectual and dissociated ("heads on sticks").

To summarize Wilber's integral theory is beyond the scope of this book (See the article The Integral Worldview on the Boulder Integral website for a short summary). But in an effort to explain why the integral community has adopted Circling with such enthusiasm, I will say the following.

The essence of the integral world-view is that all human experiences and ways of seeing the world have a "time and place", a developmental function. There is no such thing as a universal human value system or "optimal" developmental theory or right / wrong ways of being. Human history can be considered a progression from early world-views into more mature or complex or "integral" world-views (this is the theory of Spiral Dynamics, so-called "Green meme" which is allegedly our leading cultural world-view in the West, leading up to the "Mauve" or integral stages of development to which we are heading); however all of these world-views continue to have validity and applicability in certain conditions. As such, we "jump" to higher levels of development not by excluding or making-wrong where we are now or where we were at before, but by including it. This is called "Include and transcend".

How is this applicable to Circling? Because it is at the very foundation of Circling that people are the way they are for a reason, that all of us carry a piece of the puzzle, and that if we want to evolve to higher levels of social organization, of deeper caring for ourselves and for the world, we have to understand and include multiple perspectives, even perspectives that seem divergent to our core beliefs or just wrong (for instance, the perspective that either terrorists or Americans should be killed, depending on who you ask).

The ability to carry multiple simultaneous perspectives, the idea that "in relationship everyone is right", is central to the practice of Circling. I would argue that Circling is not just an extension of integral theory, it is a way to make it real and take it into the world. Circling is the most exciting thing that has happened to integral theory since its invention. Circling has moved integral theory from the position of being merely a "good idea" of uncertain applicability to world problems and even early errors and hubris (Google Mark Manson's article The Rise And Fall of Ken Wilber for an entertaining account of the early days of integral theory), into the position of being one of the best hopes that we have for our individual and collective healing and transformation. And the very *process* of how two highly disparate modalities can come together and join into a larger system, *precisely* models the change that many of us want to see, and also models integral theory itself at its best.

Surrendered Leadership and "We space"

Surrendered Leadership (SL) is the modality created at Circling Europe and used in the Avalon Community (see below). Some people think of SL as an "extension" of circling, while others think of it as a different modality, albeit one that uses Circling principles. Circling Europe certifies both Circling leaders and SL leaders.

The practice of SL involves being willing to stay in a state of not-knowing while taking total responsibility for yourself and your world. It is being willing to fully meet and embrace whatever experience you are currently having, attempting to respond from your heart. This creates an opening and a nourishing for other people to step in and be met by you.

Circling Europe describes SL as: an invitation into a form of co-created space where everyone is invited and challenged to step into their highest response-abilities and leadership, a place where people are totally free and trusted. It fosters an agile collective intelligence that absorbs the key knowledge and discernment from the group and that acts in perfect balance with what comes up and what is needed. It's a leadership that weaves together the multiple perspectives that are arising and draws out the truth and beauty at the heart of each expression. It involves a radical letting go and trust that calls forth our inspiration and creativity and opens us to the mystery and natural flow of what 'wants' to happen between us.

SL is a deep and powerful practice. It also has significant implications for social change leadership. To quote Alanja Forsberg (Avalon Dharma) in her video Surrendered Leadership - A Whole New Paradigm of Leading Groups, Teams and Organisations, the world that we are moving into will need to be co-created by us based on moment-to-moment experience, rather than an external plan or form. Thus, to become effective leaders of the future, we must let go of ideas of how things should be, and focus instead on fully showing-up to what is present.

The controversy surrounding Surrendered Leadership has less to do with the philosophy than the way it is practiced. All schools of circling agree about surrendering to what is present. Thus, all circling leaders practice some form of "surrendered leadership".

The difference is that in Circling-Europe inspired circles (SL circles), surrender is taken a step deeper, to where the facilitator may choose to no longer hold the group space as a specific structure or container. Thus, in an SL circle, there may be simultaneous multiple conversations going on in the large group, sub-groups may form spontaneously (even while you are talking!), people may express loud emotion or physicality, etc. It can look like total chaos.

(Note that this style of Circling doesn't happen – or at least not much – on the CircleAnywhere online platform. CA groups are very much like any other Circling group).

SL circles don't necessarily hold that "Yin trumps Yang". They believe that the right mix of Yin and Yang should be sought. SL circles have a (proportionately) higher value on "aliveness" (even if it looks chaotic) and less on "safety" than the style of Circling practiced in other schools.

The basic idea of SL is similar to the idea of "We space", an idea present in the Integral community for some time. "We space" practices are part of Bohm Dialogue (David Bohm), Peter Block's "a small group" (see his book Community: the Structure of Belonging), and there is a very active community called Evolutionary Collective (Patricia Albere, see below).

Circling in Business

Some of the world's top Circling leaders make most of their income through business consulting, rather than teaching Circling directly. Decker Cunov, co-founder of the Circling movement, is currently leading the charge here. Decker has a lucrative consulting practice in which he "circles" entrepreneurs, mostly Bay-area startups, and is starting to offer training in this particular modality, which is like a combination between Circling and business consulting.

Circling in business is distinct from running formal circles in a quite fundamental way, because business people and entrepreneurs won't necessarily be coming in with "connection intent" (it's the financial and relational bottom-line that preoccupies them), and it is also unlikely that they want to be educated in complex human developmental models. Thus, successfully providing business consulting services based on integral models (that include Circling) has been challenging. Decker's success in this sphere is very promising for the movement. Decker has very recently (August 2017) started teaching his business circling practice in a virtual course called "C1" (for "Consulting 101").

Business Circling has some overlap with Guerrilla Circling. In both cases, the leader or consultant will practices circling principles without declaring what they are doing and without any a-priori or explicit agreement. These principles include "getting their world", connection intent, vulnerable sharing, accurate and compassionately-delivered reflections, etc. What is different between Business Circling and Guerrilla Circling, is that in business circling there is an assumption that the "client" (circlee) will be interested in connection intent (loving and being loved) only to the extent that it serves their business purpose, for instance in creating greater alignment with their team and more powerful collaboration, or else in enlarging perspectives and surfacing blind spots. Whereas in Guerrilla Circling our assumption is that everyone simply wants to love and be loved, period, while acknowledging that this assumption may not be true in this moment.

Because of the lack of an explicit context (statement of shared values), I imagine that business circling would be quite difficult, more difficult than "formal" circling. This may be the reason that Circling still has very little penetration in business, despite the potential that many of us see there.

The truth, however, is that Circling has little penetration anywhere right now in terms of real-world problems. This is still cutting-edge work that a lot of us, including myself, are exploring.

The Yin and Yang of Circling: Connection Intent versus Developmental Intent

There exists an inescapable tension within Circling, and perhaps within all human relationships, between being non-judgmentally open and accepting to whatever is arising (the so-called "relational meditation"), and being invested or attached to certain outcomes (such as feeling a sense of connection, having a transformative conversation, or just having fun). I call this "connection intent versus developmental intent". Bryan Bayer (and others) call this "the Yin and the Yang of circling". Navigating this tension correctly is the essence of good circling.

Bryan Bayer has a model (in The Art of Circling) which I will draw from for the rest of this section. According to Bryan:

- The **Yin of Circling** (feminine aspect) is the more inclusive, embracing aspect of Circling – noticing, feeling and receiving the moment as it unfolds, with "nowhere to get to but more here". This might be the aspect of circling that primarily values "connection".
- The **Yang of Circling** (masculine aspect) is the more transcendent, active, directive and challenging – it asks penetrating questions, expresses desires, exposes patterns, seeks to achieve closure or else transformative or illuminating outcomes. This is the aspect of circling that primarily values "truth"

Bryan has a table comparing the type of processes or inquiries that each attitude will generate, and I will not repeat it here; only to say that "Yin" might include: *noticing what's present, opening up to and feeling and embracing another's experience*; while "Yang" might be more interested in *naming what is missing (the possibility of having a deeper experience or discovering more truth), drilling in, stepping outside of patterns, enlarging perspective*. These opposing and yet highly complementary attitudes might be summarized by **"I get you and I am here for you" [Yin]**, versus **"Here is what you are missing and how it could be better" [Yang]**.

The fundamental rule in circling is that **Yin trumps Yang**. I have stated this already when speaking about "connection intent". Connection is achieved primarily through Yin practices, while excessive Yang practices (such as challenging feedback that is not coming from a place of empathy and understanding) will destroy connection. However, if we *only* do Yin practices such as empathy and appreciation, while withholding our truth that we are (perhaps) bored or feeling angry, then the group will be flat and generally unsatisfactory, or worse (because when we withhold our true feelings out of fear, or obligation to be "nice", they often come out sideways and destructively later).

As always, there is no universal formula for navigating these waters. There are also some organizational preferences, with some circling schools (Integral-style circling) more focused on structure and group safety, while others (Circling Europe and Surrendered Leadership) being more willing to break the structure even at the risk of creating un-safety. A group that is too Yin (no structure) can occur as going nowhere and possibly even abusive (since lack of guidelines means that people can dump their shit on you), whereas a group that is too Yang (overly structured) can occur as awkward, over-led and disconnected. To note, however, that all schools of circling would agree that "Yin trumps Yang", so it's more a question of the *degree of intention* that leaders put into one or the other dimensions of circling. Some schools (Circling Europe in particular) are more willing to "push the envelope" in the Yin/Yang balance.

Topical Circling

"Topical Circling" is a variation of a regular circle in which we bring in more developmental intent.

It may seem that Circling is antithetical to anything that would look like goal-orientation. My experience however is the opposite, which is that in a strong circle, a circle in which everyone is aware of and is practicing circling principles to the best of their ability, development happens, sometimes extremely rapidly, and from there goals get accomplished.

The distinction between a "regular" ("relational meditation") circle and a topical circle, is that in a topical circle we hold the container more loosely. Advice and coaching are permissible (provided they are wanted), but we maintain a strong focus on the relational space and return to Yin practices if tension surfaces or if the conversation become too abstract or excessively content-focused, as in regular Circling.

Topical Circling might be considered a mix between "regular" circling ("relational meditation", no agenda except to be fully present to what is emerging) and a Mastermind group (Mastermind is a popular group structure, first mentioned in Napoleon Hill's classic [Think and Grow Rich](#)).

CHAPTER 5: COMPLEMENTARY MODALITIES

> *"We can choose to make the success of all humanity our personal business. We can choose to be audacious enough to take responsibility for the entire human family. We can choose to make our love for the World what our lives are really about. Each of us now has the opportunity, the privilege to make a difference in creating a World that works for all of us. It will require courage, audacity and heart. It is much more radical than a revolution, it is the beginning of a transformation in the quality of life on our planet. You have the power to fire a shot heard around the World."* – Werner Erhard

Circling and Authentic Relating practices have applicability to many fields, including business leadership and entrepreneurship, sexuality, trauma recovery, therapy and mental health, social change leadership, the intentional community and eco-village movement, and more. This chapter lists a few other communities and movements that overlap with circling.

Non-Violent Communication

NVC is a large and very popular movement, much better known than Circling and also (unlike Circling) with a lot of printed training resources, including Marshall Rosenberg's book <u>Nonviolent Communication: A Language of Life</u>, which has been translated into over 30 languages. NVC is also much older than Circling, since Marshall started his work in the 1960s, almost 40 years before Circling started. Marshall died in 2015, but his work continues in at least 60 countries, including many developing countries where circling has very little penetration, if at all. NVC is a fantastic resource for anyone interested in A/R and social change. In many ways, NVC is the "original" Authentic Relating model.

Circling and NVC practice groups are not vastly different. Both focus on empathy and connection. The place where Circling goes beyond NVC (and hence Circling might be considered "next generation NVC"), is in the use of impact statements and reflections, with (perhaps) a greater focus on the relational space and less focus on "techniques". The upside of Circling over NVC, is that circling can be, potentially, more exciting, deeper, and faster-paced; while the downside is that circling can devolve into a shit-storm, whereas in NVC there are "rules" and guidelines relating to responsible communication of our feelings. The idea of responsible communication is not necessarily a shared context (agreement) in circling, and because of this I have witnessed extremely inappropriate communications in circling groups (one can hope that circling is evolving and that this is happening less now).

Lastly, in terms of my compare-and-contrast of Circling and NVC, the online circling communities are very active, where in NVC most of the groups are happening on-the-ground.

Understanding Marshall Rosenberg's work, and particularly around the central function of feelings and needs, is key to effective communication, and hence to Circling skillfully. At core, NVC provides a framework and communication model for evoking, expressing and fulfilling human needs, and particularly needs for closeness, trust, authenticity and vulnerability.

The concept of "needs" is central to NVC. In NVC, *any* expression of need (provided it does not come with an unspoken judgment or demand) is considered a gift, as it gives another person an opportunity to contribute to you and hence make life more wonderful for both of you. (The idea of "making life more wonderful" is also core to NVC: our central desire, according to Marshall, being to "contribute to life").

As you become more skillful in NVC, you acquire the ability to listen for and reply empathically to the feelings and needs that underlie all human communications – even those communications that are initially expressed as judgments and demands. It is a powerful skill that can enable you to navigate successfully even the most emotionally charged and confrontational of human interactions.

The NVC concept of "needs as a gift" is revolutionary, because it is a direct contradiction to Western cultural conditioning. Most of us learn as children that needs are bad. "Needs" make us dependent on other people, vulnerable, "needy", shameful. Much better, our culture tells us, to ride solo into the sunset, masters of our own destiny, alone and above the crowd and on top of every situation. This may have been a good idea at one time, but it doesn't work anymore, not even for doing business, let alone in interpersonal relationships. In the complex and inter-related world that we live in, our true strength and power lies through connection and vulnerability. This has been confirmed in work-place studies by Google.

As such, NVC might be considered a precursor of Circling as it shares many of the same values and beliefs. NVC is an art form, like Circling and meditation, in which you can spend an entire life deepening your practice.

Authentic Man Program and Authentic Woman Experience

The Authentic Man Program (AMP) and Authentic Woman Experience (AWE) are (among other things) extensions of Circling practices into the area of dating and sexual / romantic partnership. What this means is that both programs attempt to bring greater love, authenticity and connection into romantic partnerships – an area of life which carries deep negative social conditioning and in which many of us are very troubled, hopeless and confused. This is an area of keen interest of mine and the topic of my first book, <u>As Lovers Do: Sexual and Romantic Partnership as a Path of Transformation</u>. The application of Circling and A/R connection practices to sexual relationships is very powerful, but also (like Circling for business) relatively new and cutting-edge.

AMP runs at Boulder Integral Center a few times a year and is led by Decker Cunov and team, while AWE runs in the Bay Area and is led by Alexis Shepperd and Shana James. They are both excellent programs. You can find more information on the respective websites.

The Avalon Community

The Avalon Community is a quite recent (founded by Alanja Forsberg in 2015) extension of Circling into related modalities that include psycho-drama and some form of somatic experiencing, i.e. body-centered processing and working through early trauma experiences, which would include physical touch. Their flagship offer is a retreat called "Avalon" that is 6-day, deep dive into community and, if needed, the trauma that many of us carry.

The fact of early, somatic-based trauma is, as of this year (2017) rapidly gaining weight in the circling community. There are important conversations happening, partly based of many people's experience that circling doesn't actually work for recovering from early trauma (or if it does, it is too slow). There are a number of hypotheses being offered there, one being that physical touch is essential (and is not something that normally happens during Circling, and not at all for online circling), and the second idea being that since Circling is primarily a verbal process, and since "the wounds received from relationship can only be healed in relationship", then attempting to recover from traumas inflicted at a pre-verbal age through a verbal process such as Circling may not work. As such, in an Avalon retreat, a skilled facilitator will work with a circlee, but not assume that the circlee is at a verbal age or can fully identify or express feelings, thoughts and needs. Rather, the facilitator might attempt to get into the "child's" world by asking questions such as: *how old are you? Are you angry, are you sad? Do you know what you want? Do you want me to come closer? Etc.*

I find what is currently going on in the Avalon Community intensely exciting, almost like "next-generation circling".

For more information about Avalon, look them up on Facebook under "Avalon Community" and check the website www.AvalonDharma.com

Circling, Mental Health / Addiction Recovery, and Functional Medicine

Circling has enormous applicability for mental health and addiction recovery, and especially in combination with a new type of treatment for mood disorders (and many other psychiatric diagnoses) called **Functional Medicine**.

One of the best-known proponents of Functional Medicine for the treatment of mood disorders is Kelly Brogan in her recent book, A Mind of Your Own. Kelly Brogan is a crusader for more holistic treatment of all so-called "mental health" issues, recommending diet and lifestyle changes over psychiatric medication (especially anti-depressants) as being both way more effective and safer. She has an active psychiatric practice in New York City, and is a popular blogger and "anti-pharma activist".

My partners and I are currently prototyping programs that would unite Circling, Functional Medicine, and a concept that we are calling "Cooking Collectives". The idea of a Cooking Collective is that each person in a group cooks for the others once in the cycle. So for instance a group of 5 people might agree to cook for each other at their own houses every week-day. Each person would cook once and eat 5 meals, which provides (potentially) greater quality of nutrition, economies of time and money, and community. This works best when the people in the group live close to each other (something like a community kitchen) and of course they must agree on the diet.

Circling is potentially a powerful complement to a diet- and lifestyle-based recovery program as it helps people to get into connection with each other and to form a true supportive / transformational community. We are looking for trained circling facilitators to run pilot programs, and are also exploring online circling in combination with Functional Medicine.

For more information review the website www.RelationalNutrition.com

Self-Circling, Circling Europe style

While this is not part of any official circling curriculum, Circling can be done with yourself, as an internal conversation. Daniel Tenner explains this modality:

"The way I do it, self-circling involves simply reflecting on what's happening as if there was someone in connection with me helping me explore it and probe it. Like, I might notice I feel angry. "Where is this anger? How does it feel? Is it moving?" someone might ask... so I can ask myself that too.

As I stay with the anger and observe it, I might start to discern, as I would if I was being circled, "oh, there's some pain or some fear underneath there..."

To which someone circling me would naturally respond by enquiring into that pain or that fear... so as I self-circle I will do just that... stay with the fear, discomfort, or whatever it is, hold space for it, and let it be seen for what it is, by me at least. This is less powerful than doing this with someone else - there's something about the Other that naturally makes this process better - but it can still lead to interesting place.

So then as I stay with that, say, fear, I might notice that a certain image is coming up in connection to that fear. I can then explore that image. What feelings are connected to it? What else is arising with it?

I keep digging until I decide to stop. At that point, I've usually already unpacked a whole lot of stuff and moved from reactive anger to much more self-understanding and, often, other-understanding (since often that anger might be in reaction to something outside of me, initially - or at least it feels that way).

Mostly self-circling relies on the commitment to connection with myself: being willing to stay with feelings that I'd normally want to push away or distract myself from or project onto others, to accept them, to listen to them, let them be seen and experienced fully. I think one of the most miraculous aspects of Circling is what happens when you start to do that, instead of reflexively moving away from unpleasant stuff and trying to pretend it doesn't exist.

Initially, you definitely need others to help hold space for this stuff. And, surely, I still need others to hold space for the stuff which is still too big for me to accept (and that stuff always exists somewhere I guess). But there's a lot of situations in life where I can circle myself in this way and achieve a lot of the benefits of being circled by someone else, but do it inside my head, so that by the time I communicate with the other person, what might come out is: "Wow, when you said that I got really angry. I stayed with that a bit and realized that it's because I'm afraid that you might <xyz>. Then I thought about what you said and I realize that you've already said that you wouldn't <xyz>. I guess I've not gotten over that fear of <xyz> yet. What do you think about this?" Which opens the space for a much better conversation than "wtf! Why are you doing this?"

In a sense we all do this while circling anyway - it's the bit that goes on in our self while we're silent, the reflection on "what is it that I'm actually feeling right now, authentically? What do I actually want to say?" - except that in this approach, you can just keep doing that by yourself without interacting with anyone until you feel satisfied with where you're at".

Self-Circling, IFS / IRF style

Self-circling is very complementary and a powerful addition to a popular therapy modality called **Internal Family Systems (IFS)**. The approach I am about to describe is partly derived from a similar (and very powerful) modality called **Inner Relationship Focusing (IRF)**, created by Ann Weiser Cornell; and is also related to a practice called **Voice Dialogue** (Hal and Sidra Stone), and to **Big Mind** (Genpo Roshi)

IFS posits that our psyches are composed of multiple "sub-personalities" who are often at war with each other, engaging in continuous conflict (and sometimes abuse) which lessens our effectiveness by filling our heads with arguments that never get resolved, and taking attention away from creative and constructive solutions and actions.

The solution to this problem is to "circle" your sub-personalities. The "leader" of this circle is, ideally, the "Self", or higher personality (integrating force) within the IFS model. There are various ways of doing this. You can journal in each of the sub-personalities voices. You can also do a "family meeting". I like to record my family meetings into a Digital Voice Recorder which is set on voice-activation, so I can just lie in bed relaxing and dream-up internal conversations that get recorded, and which I can listen to afterwards for relaxation or inspiration. This practice is also inspired by Shakti Gawain's book Creative Visualization, with the difference that in self-circling we are not exactly giving affirmations (although that too), we are trying to surface and lovingly resolve tensions in the inner family dynamic.

If you are doing voice dialogue and you have direct access to the sub-personality's voice, you should name that voice on the recording (i.e. "*Teenager says: fuck you, Marco*"), and then get impact statements from Self or other sub-personalities. If you don't have direct access to sub-personality voices (i.e. they communicate with you through feelings or images), then let "Self" speak for them and provide empathy, as best you can discern.

It might go something like this (I like to interject a little humor into the proceedings): "*Hello dear ones, this is your captain speaking on March 30. So, I hear some of you are pretty stressed out, and Pauline in particular is quite upset right now. I have this uncomfortable feeling in the pit of my stomach about this, and I am not sure why...*". And so forth. Try not to make anybody wrong, and when speaking as Self, position yourself as the moderator / facilitator of a circle, not the dictator of you ☺. In other words try to speak for all voices, especially the silent voices (known in IFS as "exiles") and the reactive voices (known in IFS as "protectors").

It can be quite helpful to give sub-personalities names. The first week I did this was quite exhilarating because every day a new sub-personality would emerge and get named. Naming sub-personalities is very fun, it's like a party in which every day a new arrival.

A good book to read on IFS is Jay Early's <u>Self-Therapy: A Step-By-Step Guide to Creating Wholeness and Healing Your Inner Child Using IFS, A New, Cutting-Edge Psychotherapy</u>.

Inner-Relationship Focusing (Ann Weiser Cornell)

<u>Inner Relationship Focusing</u> is a powerful self-healing practice, developed by Ann Weiser Cornell and Barbara McGavin in the early 90's. It evolved out of, and is an extension of <u>Eugene Gendlin's Focusing</u>. Gendlin's Focusing is a simple, guided <u>6-step process</u> for accessing and gaining discernment into felt-experience, and from there clearing emotional conflicts. I learned Gendlin's Focusing as a partner exercise and found it very valuable, especially since you can teach it to anyone, even a stranger, in just a few minutes (ideally however, about 10 minutes). I find Ann Weiser Cornell's work even more powerful, however, in part because it extends Gendlin's work through linguistics (NLP?), and in part because it can be done alone or as a meditation. I am also very excited to be experimenting with this practice for myself because it has some very striking similarities to Circling, and it appears to be solving some developmental issues of mine for which Circling has not really worked.

For more information see my article Inner Relationship Focusing and Circling at: <u>http://circlingguide.com/2018/01/inner-relationship-focusing-circling/</u>

Withholds, Victor Baranco style

"Withholds" are an extremely powerful communication practice, which is unfortunately not well known, and even when known is it is often misunderstood and used incorrectly, sometimes in a bad way. Withholds are not a part of the "official" Circling curriculum, but they are taught in Boulder. The Boulder Integral style of withholds is given below. The style I learned is from Victor Baranco. I am including it here because I think it is so powerful.

The goal of a withhold is to share a thought or an emotion, positive or negative, in a way that expressly and by agreement of both sides is *not* taking ownership of the feeling or experience, and hence carries an explicit request to not take it too seriously. In other words, when I say something to another person as a Withhold, for instance *"I think you are lazy"*, I am explicitly declaring that what I am about to say may have no bearing on the truth, and may not even be my own full experience, just a part of it. In essence I am sharing a thought, feeling or judgment towards another person with the explicit purpose of clearing the judgment or negative feeling and returning to a place of openness and acceptance towards them. Sharing the withhold is an attempt for me to let go of a distressing experience I am having with someone by voicing it. The other person might, if they are wise, consider the truth of my withhold and act on it (i.e. become less lazy), or not. Expressing a withhold is in no way making a demand on another person or making them wrong.

The power of withholds is that they can be a very rapid and (relatively) painless way of surfacing and then clearing tension, judgments and negative feelings in a relationship. If we don't voice the withhold, it will likely sit at the back of our mind, taking up too much of our attention and preventing us from getting into full contact or presence with the other person. Alternatively to giving the withhold, I could try and discern my true feelings and make a responsible communication, one that would own the judgment, as already discussed (i.e. rather than *"you are lazy"*, I would use correct NVC and say *"when you don't follow-up on what you agreed to do I feel angry and let down by you"*). However it sometimes takes a long time to get the degree of emotional clarity that it takes to make a responsible communication, and so (especially) with a person we love and trust, and who knows our feelings toward them, it can be more expedient to just give the withhold.

Giving a withhold is *not* usually a request to have a conversation or begin a negotiation with another person on an issue I am having with them. Rather, when used as originally designed, a withhold is a complete expression whose purpose is for me let go of a distressing emotion without requiring any response or input from the other person. However, a withhold *may* be used to begin a negotiation, i.e. as a request for collaboration around a distressing experience I am having in relationship with someone. Withholds when used in this way are a deeply integral (collaborative) practice, because the two of us together might work it out much faster and more pleasurably than me trying to do it alone. When used in this way, you will probably want to announce your intention in your withhold, as described below. Alternatively, you can agree with your partner to begin a negotiation by first clearing withholds. It is likely that the negotiation will go a lot faster and smoother if you do this. It is even possible that the process of mutually giving withholds will entirely clear the tension and there will be no need for anything more.

Practically speaking, there is a very precise structure for delivering withholds:

First, you can only do it with a person who understands the structure (since otherwise they would think that you actually believe that what you are saying about them is "true", and get defensive or reactive), and secondly, *it must be done with permission*. Asking for permission is tantamount to the difference between performing an act of love (communicating my distress with someone with an intention to clear it) and abusing them.

As such it is very important to use the following structure. You can improvise on this a little bit, by mutual agreement, but not much, if you want to be successful.

- First, say **"I have a withhold, will you hear it"**? If they don't know your meaning for "withhold", you will have to explain the structure to them another time, and deliver this particular communication differently. Also if they don't want to hear your withhold in the moment, you need to honor that.
- If they agree, you would deliver your withhold, **"You are lazy"**, or whatever. It doesn't have to be a big deal, and it can also be an appreciation or a joke, a way to clear or make light of what you perceive as their internal make-wrong, or to own and make fun of a make-wrong that you have toward them. This last use of withholds resembles what is called a

"Hex". A "hex" is something like a joke with a little "punch" to it, a grain of truth.
- The other person should respond with a simple ***"Thank you".*** This completes the cycle and you move on to other topics.
- *Withholds should not be directly responded to.* This is important and reflects the shared context that delivering a withhold does not represent any kind of "truth" (except, perhaps, a transient emotional truth in the person giving the withhold), and that the act of giving the withhold is a complete expression, not a demand the other person change
- *However,* the other person may, if they wish, either respond to a withhold with another withhold, or else ask if it's okay to have a conversation about your withhold. For instance: my response to the "you are lazy" withhold could be either to ask if you would be willing to talk about it (in case I absolutely needed to work it out with you), or else (better) to counter-withhold with an apology or even a joke ***("Thank you. I have a counter-withhold, will you hear it? Yes I know I am lazy. You should fire me")***
- An alternative structure is called "pulling withholds". Each person goes on until they are done delivering all their withholds, and then you switch roles. As mentioned above, this can be a very powerful way to begin a negotiation on a sensitive topic, and also can be a lot of fun – provided you trust and enjoy the other person.

This is the essence of Withholds. There is a more detailed description and examples of both Withholds and Hexes in my book, As Lovers Do.

Withholds, Boulder Integral style
(Post copied from a Facebook comment by Josh Levin).

1. Check your intention in wanting to share your withhold. Can you find a sincere desire to benefit the other person (in addition to yourself) and/or your connection with them? If so, proceed to step 2. If what's more true for you is that you're full of judgment/criticism/vengeance, etc, then it's not yet time to bring your withhold. Instead, it's time for a

venting session--with a trusted 3rd person, with your journal, or thru any other way you move energy/emotion.

2. Tell the person you have a withhold and tell them your "Why" for sharing it. A typical default "Why" is to get back into connection with them.

3. Ask if they are interested and available to hear it.

4. Once you get the green light, begin with this simple template:

    When you/we [name specific objective moment or experience], I felt/thought/experienced [...], and what I would've liked/would like in the future is [...].

5. Ask them to reflect back what they heard.

6. Ask them for impact from what you revealed.

7. Make any agreements that are relevant to moving forward in connection.

8. Share appreciation for doing this together.

Network For a New Culture and ZEGG

Network For a New Culture (NFNC) is a North American group inspired by the German community ZEGG.

ZEGG (which is a German acronym for "Center for Experimental Cultural Design") is an eco-village and conference center near Berlin, founded in 1991. ZEGG was originally inspired by a famous 3-year German community experiment called "Bauhütte", started in 1978 and conducted by Dieter Duhm and associates. Dieter Duhm later left ZEGG and founded the Tamera eco-village in Portugal.

ZEGG is a pioneer community practicing radical authenticity, with a particular focus on the liberation of sex and love. As such, it can be seen as an "intellectual parent" to the Circling movement, although there is no causal connection or even association at the moment between the two movements. The ZEGG community has developed practices and tools for personal expression and trust building in large groups, coming from a commitment to non-violence and to creating a more humane and loving eco-system. Their primary community-building process is called the ZEGG Forum.

The ZEGG Forum process, along with related ideas, expanded to North America as the Network for a New Culture, and has been wildly successful here with 5 different connected groups, one on the East Coast and four on the West Coast.

NFNC seeks to build a sustainable, violence-free culture through exploring intimacy, personal growth, transparency, radical honesty, equality, compassion, sexual freedom, and the power of community. NFNC believes that one of the keys to stopping the destruction of the planet is to return to the heart. They aspire to create a world where we can all be free to come from our hearts, thereby changing the culture from the inside out. NFNC facilitates events and programs designed to help heal the wounds between men and women, between men and men, women and women, the individual and the community, and between the community and the Earth.

This effort is currently pursued primarily via retreats and workshops during the year, the most significant being annual Summer Camps where what occurs is as experimental as the culture we are trying to build. At these events, there is always a clear emphasis on freedom of choice and full support of any decisions made. In other words, each individual is "at choice" to explore or not according to their own comfort level within parameters of communication designed to create "win-win" results.

NFNC events provide exciting ways to integrate new thoughts, build new relationships and get a feel for community living within a safe and stimulating atmosphere of creativity and fun. These events are designed to move participants from the conceptual directly into the experiential.

There is a great deal of overlap between the goals and practices of NFNC and Circling. They are both wonderful communities and I would like to see more interplay between the two.

Somatic Experiencing and Hakomi

Somatic Experiencing (SE) is a form of alternative therapy aimed at relieving the symptoms of post-traumatic stress disorder (PTSD) and other mental and physical trauma-related health problems by focusing on the client's perceived body sensations (or somatic experiences). It was created by trauma therapist Peter A. Levine. A very good book to read on the topic of trauma is Bessel van der Kolk's <u>The Body Keeps the Score</u>.

Another therapy modality that focusses specifically on trauma recovery is the **Hakomi Method,** which is a form of mindfulness-centered somatic psychotherapy developed by Ron Kurtz in the 1970s.

Both SE and Hakomi share the belief that trauma experiences that occur either in childhood or as adults lodge in the body, and so long as they remain unconscious, will affect our behavior and create all kinds of problems with our health, life-coping strategies, and relationships.

As discussed above in my report on the Avalon Community, trauma recovery is currently a hot topic in Circling as many people don't believe that Circling is effective for recovery from trauma experiences, and can even be damaging, by the simple fact that Circling is by its nature a peer-led movement, and so leaders and participants may lack knowledge or expertise in dealing effectively with people carrying deep trauma, and may re-trigger the circlee unawarely. This actually occurs quite frequently. As such there are situations where a somatic-based therapy modality may be very helpful, either as a substitute for circling or as an addition. Circling does have the capacity to provide a peer environment meeting contact needs, a social support network such as no therapy modality could ever provide (it would cost too much, to begin), and as such I would recommend both Circling *and* therapy for people dealing with trauma experiences.

Adult Attachment Theory

Circling can be very powerful in contributing to an already established way of thinking about relationships called Adult Attachment Theory. Adult Attachment Theory is a branch of psychology that says that the early experiences between parent and child create working models of relationships that, without reflection, an adult will carry with them for their entire lives. Marenka Cerny, who is a somatic psychotherapist practicing Circling for a few years with Guy Sengstock, recognized that the substantial benefits of immersion in Circling are in many ways the same as when someone is, what is known as, "securely attached".

In her article, <u>A New Development in Psychology: Adult Secure Attachment and Circling</u>, Marenka points to the significant distinctions between secure and insecure attachment. She wrote, "adults who are insecurely attached will frequently exhibit recurring negative behaviors in relationship: the tendencies to avoid other people, to be critical, controlling, insensitive, readily show anger and fear, and, to deny one's own needs. Basically, an adult with insecure attachment will frequently either not clearly recognize their own needs, or the other person's, or both." By contrast, "securely attached adults have a greater capacity to trust others, tolerate conflict, and exercise discernment when forming new bonds. They are empathetic, and know how to set and sustain appropriate boundaries as they cultivate meaningful connections with others."

Marenka has been working to articulate the connection between Circling and Adult Attachment Theory, and she is currently working on her third essay on the topic. She has proposed that "Circling creates the conditions to experience what secure attachment feels like even before attachment wounds are healed," sometimes even the first time a person circles. For anyone interested in this thesis, Marenka has an important caveat: "Circling by itself does not develop secure attachment, nothing creates secure attachment without a person's intention to heal their attachment wounds." But, she also suggests, "since Circling generates *the feelings and mindstate* of secure attachment with peers — by engendering the emotional and psychological clarity between people that occurs in securely attached relationships — then if one circles regularly, perhaps in conjunction with psychotherapy," it is possible that "secure attachment can be expedited more efficiently than with psychotherapy alone."

For more information, Google the article: A New Development in Psychology: Adult Secure Attachment and Circling by Mařenka Cerny.

The Evolutionary Relationships Movement (Patricia Albere)

There are many groups currently exploring the concept of "evolutionary relationships". One of the basic ideas there is that we have outgrown individual methods of spiritual growth, including meditation, individual therapy, or body/mind practices such as Yoga, and are being called to something else, a type of "mutual awakening", or to "waking up together".

One of the most active of these groups is the Evolutionary Collective. To quote Patricia Albere, founder of this school: "Millions of us, at this point, have done sufficient amounts of personal spiritual work and individual development and are ready to move to the next stage of awakening for humanity. Some have called it a new stage of human evolution altogether, which is moving from self-reflective, individual self-concern to an awareness of self that is more fluid, interpenetrating, simultaneously aware of self and other. We know that Unity consciousness is real, many of us have had individual momentary experiences that have changed our lives. It's now time to enter into the experience of unity by awakening and living it together. We can access unity and live not only from a powerful sense of connectedness, but also, a surprisingly increased experience of our uniqueness".

For more information, see www.EvolutionaryCollective.com, or read Patricia's new book, Evolutionary Relationships.

Sociocracy

This chapter would not be complete without mentioning an organizational governance model called **Sociocracy**, which is deeply complementary to Circling, and has enormous applicability and importance in the field of organizational development.

Sociocracy can be summarized as:

- A social ideal that values equality and the rights of people to decide the conditions under which they live and work, and
- An effective method of organizing collaborative and productive organizations as associations, businesses, and governments, large and small.

In English-speaking countries, as a method of organization sociocracy is often called dynamic governance, but around the world is simply called sociocracy. Its founder called it the Sociocratic Circle-Organization Method (SCM).

Sociocracy is a whole-systems approach to designing and leading organizations. It is based on principles, methods, and a structure that creates a resilient and coherent system. It uses transparency, inclusiveness, and accountability to increase harmony, effectiveness, and productivity. Sociocracy both *enforces* we-space processes at the level of organization, and *requires* that individuals understand and practice we-space principles in order for it to be effective. As such it is highly complementary to Circling and Surrendered Leadership practices.

Sociocracy is rapidly gaining adoption, especially in organizations with a goal towards social change or conscious business. There are many online and printed resources available, including www.Sociocracy.info. Also check out We the People: Consenting to a Deeper Democracy, by John A. Buck.

Other compatible modalities

In addition to the above, the following groups are pursuing research and running programs that could be considered highly complementary to Circling, and/or to evolutionary relationships:

- Saniel Bonder's <u>Waking Down in Mutuality</u>
- Robert Augustus Masters <u>To Be a Man</u>, and other books
- Keith Witt, and Martin Ucik: <u>Integral Relationships: A Manual for Men</u>
- Eivind Figenschau Skjellum's <u>Reclaim Your Inner Throne</u>
- Pacific Integral's Causal Leadership
- Diane Hamilton and Rob McNamara's Integral Facilitator Training
- Christian Pankhurst's Heart IQ
- Thomas Hübl's teachings on awakening in relationships
- Lonneke van Elburg
- Lynn Kreaden
- Lynne McTaggart <u>The Power of 8</u>

CHAPTER 6: NEXT STEPS

> *"Enlightenment is when you realize that what was planned was a party"* -- Victor Baranco

So we get to the end of this book – Eureka! – and to the very practical question: *Okay, this is very cool. What next?*

The first step, obviously, is to attend a circle or an Authentic Relating (A/R) game night, ideally in your community, but online works well as well. It is not necessary to be formally trained in Circling in order to join a group and start to circle, however it is always helpful to take an introduction to circling class. These are offered regularly in many cities that have A/R communities, and also online (especially on Circle Anywhere). Your best bet to find such a class would be to consult the communities map at www.authrev.com and from there write to the organizers of the community where you reside, if you can find one.

It can take a little while to really "grok" the circling practice and begin to be effective. When I say "effective", I mean to the point where you can actually express leadership in a circle (and remember that everyone in a circle is potentially a leader, the way to "leadership" is simply to practice good attention, empathy and vulnerable sharing). Some people with little previous experience can "drop in" immediately into the circling container and become effective leaders right away. Others might take a few months or longer. I was about 3-4 months circling before I could begin to say I "got it" and I could, most of the time (not always!), express effective leadership (this is slightly embarrassing to say, as I had previously 30 years of therapy and other developmental work before I started circling, which included founding and running an intentional community). Some people might take years to really "get" circling. It's not a "magic bullet" to love, community, and personality integration. But regardless of whatever level you start at in terms of emotional self-awareness, empathy, and presence, it is certain that Circling is going to be a lifetime developmental journey. I don't believe that development would ever stop, in my case. It is truly an "infinite game".

As you would expect, your best access to high-level circling skills is to actually circle with skilled facilitators, either on-the-ground in your community or on the online platforms. Online circling is surprisingly fun and effective, I have built lifetime friendships and collaborators from it in a very short time, and I strongly recommend it if you are serious about becoming a relational leader.

Good luck! Write to me your inspiring stories to marc@CirclingGuide.com, and I may post them, with your permission!

Facilitation of Circles, and Running Private Circles

Once you start to feel effective in circling, most of the time, I would strongly encourage you to start your own groups, either in person or online. You don't need a certificate or years of training to do this. Of course training can help, but you don't actually need it, and particularly if you start circling with your friends and business collaborators. All you really need to circle effectively is to practice the basic principles as outlined in this book, the core of which *are curiosity, empathy, appreciation, vulnerable sharing and "non-doing".* It's not exactly rocket-science, and there are not really any "experts" either, as even the best of us get triggered sometimes and do or say stupid or unskillful things.

There is no better developmental practice than running your own groups – and especially with your friends, who might be initially resistant to your leadership and want to relate to you in old ways, ways that they have come to know you. Do not be surprised or disappointed if this happens, it is inevitable and will ultimately challenge you to even greater skill as a relational leader.

You can check the **Leader Formats** chapter for ideas and formats for leading A/R Games and Circles.

Please join the Circling Guide community!

You may join our community at www.CirclingGuide.com, which will bring you news of cutting-edge circling developments, along with offers from me and the community. You can also find me on Facebook at: facebook.com/CirclingGuide

ARTICLES AND STORIES

> *"It is no measure of health to be well adjusted to a profoundly sick society"* – *Jiddu Krishnamurti*

(This chapter should be considered a "stub". Please share your inspirational story to marc@CirclingGuide.com!)

What is authenticity? (Sara Ness)

Sara Ness is a legend in the Circling and A/R movement. She is the director of Authentic Revolution, lead facilitator on Authentic World, author of The Authentic Relating Games Manual, and creator of the Authentic Life Leadership Course, a live course which runs in approximately 2 months cycles and is highly recommended.

Is it total honesty in all your words and actions? Is it following your impulses, your emotions, or your beliefs? Is it a popular word that writers use to get more hits on Google? As far as I can tell, it depends on who you ask. I asked the internet, since it was the closest thing to me while I was writing this. The first two definitions that came up were "authenticity is the quality of being authentic" - very helpful - and, thanks to Merriam-Webster, authenticity is being "true to one's own personality, spirit, or character".

Let's break this down. There are actually **two parts to this definition: one, what is "being true" and two, what is "personality, spirit, or character".** If we see "being true" as showing a self to the world that is an accurate model of your internal thoughts, feelings, and beliefs, authenticity is what I'd call congruence - alignment between who you are and what you show.

But, who are you? What is personality, spirit, or character?

I don't know about you, but **when I look within for the truth about who I am, I come up with ten different answers.** Even right now, who am I? If who I am is affected by what I experience and how I experience it, I could start by asking myself, how am I experiencing my reality right now? The first thing I notice is that I feel a lot of energy in my body. But what does that mean about me? Am I a highly motivated and energized person? Or simply a caffeinated person? Or am I one who is anxious? Or excited? The same exact sensations could lead to multiple different interpretations of who I am. And how I act and communicate will be affected by which truth I choose.

I recently listened to a TED talk by Kelly McGonigal, the author of 'Reality is Broken', one of my favorite books on gamifying the world around us. Kelly cites a study that tracked the relationship between stress and death. Experiencing major stress within the past year conferred a 43 percent higher risk of death - but *only* for those who said they thought stress was harmful to their health. Some people interpret the physical symptoms of stress - faster breathing, heart pounding, focused mind - as energy or intensity and experience their body readying itself to face a challenge. Those who viewed stress in this way - as helpful - had no higher risk of dying than those who had not experienced major stress in the last year.

Forty-three percent higher risk - or zero percent higher risk - all depending on how we define a single experience. And we do this all the time! We put interpretations on what we think, feel and perceive; we filter through hundreds of different possible responses to any situation, and try to find which version holds the most truth, or is the most authentic, for us.

But **what if all of our possible responses are authentic**? They all come from different internal parts of us, each of which has reason to believe and feel what it experiences. Right now, part of me says "You should pause here and re-write this script. It isn't good enough." Another part says "Act confident! You can't serve people if they think you don't trust yourself." Another part says, "I'm tired. Maybe I should take a break."

Which of these parts is most authentic? The first, which wants me to stop and re-write the script, is true to my fear of being seen as incompetent and my value on doing really good work. The second part, which wants me to act confident, is true to my feeling of competency and my belief that people trust confidence more than admissions of vulnerability (a belief which an old part of me believes strongly and a newer part of me questions). The third part, who is just tired, is almost always there. It's like the whiny kid dragging on my heels: "Are we done yet?" That part is really good at justifying procrastination, "But it's authentic, you want to procrastinate!" If my goal is to live and lead from authenticity, how do I choose which part to listen to and when?

Here's where we find congruence. Congruence is alignment between who you are and who you show the world. I've just put forth the idea that our self is made up of many selves, each of which has its own version of truth, influenced by the words we choose to describe our experience. So if I have to choose how I will show up to the outside world, I need to decide between these selves. For me, I make this decision using my values.

My values are the things I care most about. You may know your own core values, or they may be a mystery. We'll do an exercise this week to help you discover or clarify the ones that are most important to you. When you know your values, you can check decisions against them, especially a decision like which part of myself do I follow in this moment, and which part do I show the world? Once your values are deeply internalized, you don't even need to check. You'll find yourself making decisions easily and congruently without thinking about it.

Learning moves from unconscious incompetence, to conscious incompetence, to conscious competence, to unconscious competence. Congruent authenticity is a learned skill. In the beginning, we need to bring a whole lot of self-awareness to our most essential values, and then practice consciously choosing to show the world who we really are and what we really value. By doing so over time, our values will eventually become deeply internalized. This is what I'm calling unconscious congruence. Once we develop unconscious congruence, we spend less energy worrying about what parts of ourselves to show the world, and we have more energy for fully living our authentic life.

In summary, to be authentic, we first have to sort out who we are and what really matters to us, and then sort out how to bring our words, actions, and choices into congruence with our values.

To have others receive and validate our authenticity, we need to make the environment around us safe enough to share ourselves vulnerably. This means developing an awareness of others' modes of communication, the frames through which they see the world, which may be similar or very different from our own. We'll use Authentic Relating to give tools and practices that can streamline this congruent communication. We'll also work on developing emotional resilience for those moments in which our authenticity isn't received, and learn to face the "boss battles" of relating with those who don't want to accept us for who we are.

Congruent authenticity is a skill you can master. And once you do so, even if it's awkward at first - as learning any new skill is - you will start to find much more ease and satisfaction in the connections you care most about, and those you have every day.

Beyond Circling: I have a dream (Marc Beneteau)

In an earlier blog post I gave some of the reasons why I am so passionate (read: obsessed) with Circling. To bottom-line that post, I have spent 30+ years looking for a community-based healing movement, a "transformational tribe", that would meet the following criteria: power or effectiveness; integrity; free or low-cost; a global reach; and a compelling vision for a new society. In those 30 years, nothing was able to meet all those criteria, until I stumbled across Circling. Furthermore, it quickly became obvious to me that Authentic Relating practices were the "missing link" from virtually *every* ashram or meditation or yoga center, every social change movement, and almost every other human transformational system (with the exception of NVC, which I consider a close cousin but earlier generation of Authentic Relating). Indeed: if you truly want to experience the depth of human fucked-up-ness, go into most any Ashram or yoga center and ask the teachers, confidentially, what they think of the organization. I don't mean that Yoga philosophy or Buddhism or anything else is wrong. I just mean that without authentic relating, they will forever be missing something. At least that's my opinion.

Now I want to continue that article with a sequel giving what I have learned in 8 months of circling 10 or 12 hours a week, first in Boulder and later on the online platforms, [Circle Anywhere](#) and [Authentic World](#). And talk about where I want to go with this.

Despite 30 years of my fascination and research into human development, emotional communication and the psychology of love, and intentional communities / eco-villages, it still took me quite a while to even begin to "get" circling. In the first few months I was like a bull in a china shop. I enjoyed almost every minute of it, and had some very powerful birthday circles in Boulder, but the people around me did not always enjoy me. It took me quite some time to accurately frame how I was being (and declare myself publicly) as a "recovering asshole". Not always of course, as people did enjoy my vulnerability (this is my super-power), but despite my best intentions that was often the truth. It was hard to contain my own reactivity and I am not one to keep my opinions to myself. It also took me a while to understand what some people considered my excessive tendency to story-telling. Sometimes I would respond with humor, as in "look. I am Jewish and Italian, I like to talk".

There were two inflection points in this exhilarating journey. I say "exhilarating" because it was clear to me from the very beginning that I was on to something very powerful.

The first inflection point occurred about 4 months into it when I started inviting people I liked into private groups held over Zoom. The stated purposes for this was, first to introduce circling to my non-circling friends (who would be more willing, the argument went, to join free groups); second that the private group format provided more continuity and trust; and third I wanted to introduce more of what I called "developmental intent", which I say more about below.

The first objective, of introducing my friends to circling, mostly failed. Granted, a few of my friends took to it like fish-to-water and now more-or-less share my enthusiasm, so I am not a complete loser as a circling evangelist. Still this is a bit disappointing.

The second and third objectives were very successful, however. People loved the private groups, often had important experiences there and kept coming back. Ultimately I realized something which I think is important. Certainly there is something to be said for a group that has commitment, continuity and trust. But that alone does not explain the success of the private groups. I mean, I can show up to most any Circle Anywhere group and feel love and trust towards people there as well, in addition to skilled leadership, something that every aspiring leader ought to relish, the revealing of one's blind spots. CA has become my new family-of-choice. But what I realized was that **the key factor in the transformative power of the private groups is that these groups extended circling into the realms of friendship, true transformational (or healing) partnerships, and in a few cases business collaboration.** This is what I mean by "developmental intent". "Relational meditation" is well and good, I have no objections. But if we limit our circling to the formal groups, that to me misses the whole point and the greater power to be gained from the practice.

And this realization was the first inflection point in my circling "career". The fulfillment, as it were, of my original intention which was to bring circling into the world: into friendships, into families, into schools and business, into other types of transformational tribes — there is NO human community of any kind, in my opinion, that could not benefit from this.

And yet I have found that bringing Circling or A/R practices into the world to be challenging. My attempts to lead groups (or even individual sessions) to people who are not already trained in Circling have been hit-or-miss (as opposed to the private groups, almost all of which have been home runs). Why is this? Well, I can't say for sure of course and this is certainly in part a reflection on my leadership. And yet it is also logical that this would be true. Because of the 4-5 primary skills of Circling, in my world (curiosity, empathy, appreciation, vulnerable sharing and "non-doing"), none of them are easy, and in all cases the "social rules" are stacked up against us ("*don't stare at strangers*" — oh really. Why?). **But the hardest of all is vulnerable sharing,**

which is something that many people are simply terrified of doing. And it's not just terror that stops them from doing it, it's that they can't even imagine the benefits that lie on the other side of it. In truth, **vulnerable sharing is a revolutionary act**. And for those people who don't get it, or don't want to do it, I can only model it. In most cases they will respond very positively (vulnerability is very attractive), but in other cases they won't. And I have to be strong enough to endure that, what I call the "judgments of the world". Because when I show up in vulnerable sharing, I am also revealing my own neuroses. Which, if you know me, are rather self-evident. "Recovering asshole" is actually the least of them. From my perspective, what chance do I have of becoming less neurotic if I have to hide? I have always thought of vulnerability as a no-brainer, but I seem to be in the minority there.

Now let me give the second inflection point of my circling career.

It's that Circling alone is not enough, and particularly in designated groups. There are some limits of the developmental value of "relational meditation". There are fewer limits of bringing circling into friendship, transformational partnerships, intentional communities and business, which is what I am most interested in, but there are limits even there. Circling alone, I have found (and there are big conversations happening there on Facebook) is not that effective for healing trauma, for that one needs somatic (body-centered) therapy modalities like Somatic Experiencing, Hakomi, or Avalon. It's not very effective, in my experience, for addiction recovery either. I was an active alcoholic for about three years, even as I was going through my circling adventures. Nothing changed there until I started looking at and complementing my Circling with other modalities, such as Inner Relationship Focusing and re-connected to 12-step support communities.

Ultimately what I am saying is that I still think that circling is incredible. But I am slightly sobered-up. I am no longer claiming it as the solution to anything-that-ails-you. However, I will continue to claim that at least for me, and probably for a lot of other people as well, it is, perhaps, the **first step** to the solution of anything-that-ails-you. Human beings thrive on connection, and without connection they perish. That's my story and I am sticking to it. I am also out to prove it. I am out to prove that almost anyone will respond positively to the fundamental skills of circling (curiosity, empathy, appreciation, and vulnerable sharing), 90% of the time. I want to go out into the world and practice, and watch people transform around me, as is already starting to happen (I hope), and at very minimum is happening with me.

I think of this as a very important conversation. Can we, actually, expand Circling beyond the "relational meditation", without killing it, or destroying the purity that may be the very reason for its success? What are your thoughts on this? Please post them to Circling Guide on facebook.

Selling Authentic Relating, Part 2 (Marc Beneteau)

Summary

It's a strange thing: the more I circle, and lead circling, the more excited and engaged I am about the potential of the modality and of the movement. In this article I take a step back and try and discern why this is so, along with some practical approaches for promoting A/R and Circling events and building a community.

My Circling Manifesto (where I think this is heading)

I say this here, even though it's something that I consistently fail to convince anyone, until they have actually attended a Circle (and even then. Most people fail to get the social and political implications of the movement, in my view). I have spent 30+ years exploring human change modalities, looking for something that would be (a) powerful (or effective), (b) open-source, (c) low-cost, (d) that would have sexual and financial integrity, and (e) would have a global presence and community (i.e. a possibility for anyone anywhere on Earth to join a group or start a group). 98% of human change systems fail one or more of those tests, mostly because they are proprietary (or brand-controlled), and/or have limited reach. The 2% which do pass these tests, which include Buddhism and NVC, derive much of their effectiveness by harnessing the power of group intelligence. This is the central point of Circling and

A/R practices, its specialty shall we say. And I have not seen any movement or group, proprietary or not, harness the group intelligence for transformational purposes as well as Circling does. Or that is anywhere near as fun, frankly.

And furthermore, Circling and A/R practices are very easy to sell. I mean: the impossibility of adequately explaining the practice, is more than compensated by the dramatic impact that I have seen from people attending even a *single event*. Whether you are leading A/R games or Circling, and assuming a certain skill level, it is very common to see people leaving a group very inspired, what I call the "home-run circle" (everyone leaves happy and smiling and wanting more). In terms of "skill level" — well just how much skill level is required I have yet to discover, but I don't feel that any of this is rocket-science. I am far from being the best leader in the world, and yet I think I am having really good impact.

And finally — as if all this were not enough — *Circling is a perfect complement to most any intentional community, any ashram or church or spiritual community, any mind/body transformation program, any social-change movement, any addiction or mental-health recovery program, or any conscious business venture.* I call it the "missing link" — without it, you will forever be missing something. It doesn't matter how powerful the underlying philosophy or modality is. If you are not dealing with relational reality, you are fucked. Very few communities or social-change organizations are adequately dealing with relational reality. Why? Because, in general, it's a swamp. Better (a lot of people think) to just ignore it, since fully locking-in to emotional and relational truth, communicating lovingly and responsibly around that and fully owning your emotional experience, can be dangerous. Things can get very hot very fast. Relationships and entire organizations can blow apart. In essence, most of us are still babies in the art of relationship. Our parents didn't teach us and society does everything possible to shut us up. We are basically "learning on the job", even the most skillful of us. Being authentic and loving at the same time is very difficult. *But the alternative, which is to live inside a lie, is generally worse.*

For sure, I am a Circling fanatic. I imagine I could Circle all day long and be perfectly happy. So perhaps I am not the best person to bring a balanced opinion to bear here. *"Multiple simultaneous perspectives"* — no argument. There have been a number of recent scandals rock the Circling world. Even so: my desire is to see more people in the Circling community claim their power here, and start to lead, especially locally. We are on to something, folks. Something that the world desperately needs, and which not many others are bringing.

Selling A/R, 1-2-3

I want to expand on the above, as per my previous article Love for Sale, Half-Price, *on how easy it is to sell Authentic Relating.* There is not a lot of money in it, at least at the beginning. But the personal and social value-added is so extraordinary, it's worth doing regardless, in my view. My desire for myself, is to lead on-the-ground every night. Why not? It's super-fun for me, I have a lot of time on my hands, I am pretty good at it (or at least "good enough"), and I could use the money. My plan for "filling seats" is to reach out to other Meetup organizers and compatible organizations (co-working spaces for instance). Personally, I have a deep desire and am very passionate about intentional community, residential or not (as told in my personal blog post Moving to Asheville, and other news), so that is also on the agenda. I am very interested in expanding A/R and Circling practices into real-world scenarios that would include intentional community and eco-villages, mental health and addiction recovery, sexuality, and conscious business. This is my life's work.

Where to go from here?

Creating a thriving A/R community in your locality is challenging, for reasons already mentioned: *human relationships are a swamp.* Especially when questions of money, power, prestige and sex start to come in. I will still passionately declare, that it is a game worth playing.

Here are some good resources for learning A/R skills and building community:

- Circleanywhere. The best-value Circling training on the planet. Authentic World is also good but doesn't have the same level of activity. There are (sometimes) free groups offered by Daniel T. Johnson and by Josh Stein.
- Sara Ness's new community course [link needed]
- Jordan Allen's community course [link needed]
- The expanded Circling Guide, which includes updated A/R Game Leader Format and Circling Introduction Leader Format
- Local Circling and A/R groups, which you can generally find on Meetup.com
- Finally, you can always post and look for support on Circling Europe Facebook, Authentic Relating Event Facilitators, Circling Community Facebook, Circling Facebook, Circling and A/R for Organizations, CircleAnywhere Facebook, Authentic World Members. As well as Facebook pages for your local community.

RESOURCES

Below you will find links and resources relating to Circling and the Authentic Relating movement. This section should also give you some ideas about where to start, and ideas for starting your own groups, in person or online.

For finding a group in your area, your best bet is to look at the communities map at https://www.authrev.com/worldwide-connection/. You can also look for compatible groups on Meetup.com, such as NVC.

Training Organizations

In addition to local communities, all of which offer either Circling intros or Authentic Relating Games nights, the organizations below offer advanced training in Circling, at different locations and/or online.

Lineage Circling schools

The three "primary lineage" schools of Circling are as follows (in order of creation):

- **CIRCLING INSTITUTE** (San Francisco CA, Asheville NC, Washington DC and other places), CirclingInstitute.com. Led by Guy Sengstock and team.
- **INTEGRAL CENTER** (Boulder, Colorado), IntegralCenter.org. Pioneered by Decker Cunov and today led by Robert MacNaughton, with contributions from Michael Porcelli, Josh Levin, Jess Nichol, and many others. (Update February/2018: The physical location of the Boulder Integral Center is shutting down. T3 program will continue. Other activities are currently under discussion).
- **CIRCLING EUROPE** (Amsterdam & Western Europe/Norway, New York City, Austin TX, and other places), CirclingEurope.com. Led by John Thompson, Sean Wilkinson and Jordan Myska Allen

Other Circling and A/R Training Organizations

- **AUTHENTIC REVOLUTION** (Austin TX, Boston, and other places). www.authrev.com. Led by Sara Ness and team. This is the most active "non-lineage" school running training in both A/R Games facilitation, high-level circling skills, and community gatherings in the Austin area.
- **THE CONNECTION MOVEMENT** (New York City and online). TheConnectionMovement.com. Led by Amy Silverman and team.
- **ART INTERNATIONAL** (AuthenticRelatingTraining.com). Led by Jason Digges and Ryel Kestano, and offering A/R leadership facilitation in New York City, North Africa, and other places.
- **THE SCHOOL OF CIRCLING WIZARDRY** (Toronto, Ontario, and online), circlingwizardry.com. Led by Josh Stein.

Online Circling

You join online circling with a computer equipped with a webcam, or even on your phone. *Online Circling and A/R games are surprisingly effective and highly recommended.*

- **Circle Anywhere** (www.circleanywhere.com). A product of Circling Europe and operating since 2015. CircleAnywhere is the largest online circling community, with 20+ sessions every week, skilled facilitation and relatively small group size (limit is 18 participants per circle, which translates into two breakouts of 9 people). And at $50/mth for unlimited circling, the price is a steal (compare to the cost of therapy, which may not even be as effective!)
- **Authentic World** (www.authenticworld.com) is currently the hub of online circling, online A/R games, and cutting-edge circling theory for the Austin & Boulder Integral crowd. It's not as active as CircleAnywhere, but the price of $25/mth is also a steal.

Books, articles and podcasts about Circling

There are a few books on Circling, listed below, and a lot of podcasts that cover similar material. Below is a very short list. You can find more on the Resources section of www.CirclingGuide.com.

- The Art of Circling: 37 Practices for Deepening Your Relating Skills, by Bryan Bayer. Published September 2014 on Lulu. 105 Pages, $24 USD.
- The Art of Getting Someone's World + Guide to Soul-Bending, by Sara Ness. Self-published at https://www.authrev.com/circling-resources/. 33 Pages, Price by donation. The website has other great resources and interviews as well.
- Cohering the Integral We Space: Engaging Collective Emergence, Wisdom and Healing in Groups. This is a collection, of which Chapter 15: We-Space Practice, the Future, Circling and All There Is is an article by Sean Wilkinson and John Thompson, founders of Circle Europe. Available on Amazon and Kindle from $10 USD.
- Millennials, Here's Why You're Dissatisfied At Work. Article in Forbes with Sean Wilkinson, John Thompson, and Jordan Myska Allen. See also the Unconventional Life podcast (www.unconventionallifeshow.com) interview with Sean, John and Jordan.

Differences in the various schools of Circling

Joshua Zader's view

The following comments are re-posted from an article by Joshua Zader. [Work-in-progress]

After having spent at least a long weekend training in each tradition — and talking with folks like Sara Ness and Michael Blas, who are deeply trained in multiple traditions — here are my reflections on their varying emphases.

If I were to pick one word to describe the top priority of each tradition, it would be "technique" for the Integral Center, "heart" for the Circling Institute, and "presence" for Circling Europe.

More observations, somewhat off-the-cuff:

- The Integral Center and Circling Institute both prioritize birthday circles (where the focus of attention remains with one person for the duration of the circle), in contrast to organic circles (where the group's attention moves freely from one participant to another, depending on what arises).

- Circling Europe emphasizes a more meditative and presence-oriented style of circling, often in an advanced form of organic circles they call "surrendered leadership" circles. There is no designated facilitator, and yet experienced participants do very distinctly model the kind of presence, vulnerability, and self-awareness they hope to see — exerting a different kind of influence on the group. You lead by embodiment, rather than authority.

- All three schools are heavily influenced by the Integral philosophy. The leaders of the Circling Institute seem additionally influenced by A.H. Almaas's Diamond Heart system, though I'm not confident if that shows up in circles, per se. (I'd love to learn, because I respect his work.)

- Two phrases I hear often from Integral Center trainees are "Yin wins" (meaning, if you're ever uncertain about whether to choose a more penetrative vs. receptive intention, go with receptive) and the pithy "Welcome everything, assume nothing."

- The Circling Europe style leaves far more space for conflict. To an extent, this is in the nature of organic circles, where more voices are active. But they also place a strong emphasis on trusting one's experience; and when two people have divergent perspectives, and they're both trusting their experience, it can get intense quickly. It can also lead to profound depth of insight and connection.

- The Austin community has developed its own integrative, casual, community-oriented approach, including a "hot tub" style of organic circling where there is no facilitator and little emphasis on technique. Sometimes no one in a circle is a trained circling facilitator. But there is a strong shared bias toward care and ownership of experience, which contributes to the feeling of circling.

- To my lights, Circling Europe has the most uncompromising emphasis on spiritual growth. But getting there requires a high tolerance for uncertainty, conflict, and intense self-reflection.

- If I knew I wanted to bring circling into a school, business, or other organization, I would almost certainly seek training in the Circling Institute or Integral Center traditions, where there is more structure and you're trained to give newcomers more explicit guidance.

- The Integral Center trains skilled facilitators. Circling Europe trains awakened beings. Circling Institute trains _____. (Empaths? This is the tradition I've studied in least, so far. So I'm unsure.) Obviously these aren't mutually exclusive, but they seem to reflect strong internal priorities among the leadership.

Josh Stein's view

(From a post by Josh Stein, founder of the School of Circling Wizardry)

I have trained extensively with the Integral Center (IC) and Circling Europe (CE). I have much less exposure to the Circling Institute (CI) so I'll have less to say.

No school is perfect; each does some things really well, and each has significant failings. My hope is that we will all get better at producing many skillful and even a few masterful Circlers.

Note, it's been a few years since I've trained with IC and CE, so I expect things have already improved.

Integral Center: great at teaching the techniques and framework that point to the essence of the part of Circling that is getting one's world. Unfortunately, the emphasis on doing the techniques right can suck the life out of the experience of alive with-ness. As a result, in extreme cases Circles can feel flat, tight, or analytical.

Circling Europe: great at the aliveness element, embodiment is HUGE, and emphasizing self trust in a way that makes it more likely for students to find their being'ness. CE circles are richly alive IMO. My Circling has benefited so much from CE. On the downside, their contexting and level of instruction has been weak in the past. They are amazing at modeling and transmitting Circling, AND I have wanted to see them to improve on teaching their students a framework and guiding them in developing specific skills. The lack of context is more of a concern for newbie Circlers. (However, since writing this, I have been assured that CE has upped its standards and context setting has been improved.) If I were running CE, I would want SAS to be considered an advanced course for previously trained facilitators. Surrendered Leadership Circling is an incredible practice IMO, but some people are hesitant to call it Circling because it does not always resemble and sometimes seems to break the rules of traditional Circling.

Circling Institute (my impressions): strong theoretical framework (and breaking the skill sets down into underlying components) and strong on caring and togetherness. Downsides are that the lines get blurred between Circling and therapy. Sometimes it seems there's a bias towards helping circlees move past their experience rather than truly being with it. That said, this feels like a grey area to me and I'd like to see it closer up. I'd consider taking AoC if it were practical for me.

Michael Porcelli's view
See http://integralcenter.org/3-schools-circling/

LEADER FORMATS

> *"Walk cheerfully over the world, answering that of God in every one"* – George Fox

Summary of the Leader Formats

In this section I offer an **A/R Game Format** and a **Circling Introduction Leader Format** that have worked very well for me in a group size of between 6 and 10 participants in a 2 hour meeting. The A/R game is a type of Hot Seat game, and for the Circle I am proposing short birthday circles for everyone, or as many as can fit. Be aware that 10 participants is stretching the game in terms of the time that each participant has, you will have to be disciplined with the time. If there are more than 9 or 10 participants, you may need to try something other than presented here.

The ultimate resource on A/R Games is Sara Ness's [Authentic Relating Games Manual](). I am going to go more granular here, presenting the exact language and format that I have used successfully.

Overall leadership guidelines

It is normal to be nervous when you start leading. My advice is as follows:

- DO be transparent. This is the best thing you can do, and actually the *only* way you will be successful as an A/R leader. You have to "practice what you preach". Share your nervousness, and also vulnerably-share any challenges you are having, i.e. *"I feel like I am trying too hard to make something happen here"*. I am *always* nervous leading a new group, yet I frequently get strong feedback at the end of how much people value my leadership.
- DO be very aggressive on the appreciations. Sincere appreciations will have an impact on the group way beyond what you imagine, plus of course they will start modeling you. If you feel the group is very present or mature, if

anybody demonstrates real empathy or expresses leadership, or you see anything at all that makes you feel warm or smiley, SAY IT.

- DON'T talk too much. A spoken intro should be no more than 5 minutes. This is the #1 mistake I see leaders making, even experienced ones. It's highly unlikely that people are there to hear you talk! Give them an immediate experience of connection with each other, instead. It's not very difficult and will be way more fun for them.

- DO frequent popcorn-style impact or reflection rounds. Tell them: *"we are going to do an impact round now"*. They will be curious about "impact", so explain to them: *"it's an opportunity to share your felt experience about what just happened or where you are at right now"*.

- DON'T be shy about giving negative feedback or redirects. Just do it respectfully and with permission. This happens most commonly when people are giving advice, coaching or excessive personal story-telling on an impact/reflection round. Say: *"Can I challenge you on something, is it okay?"* And after permission: *"that felt more about you than about her. Do you agree? Would you be willing to try that again?"*. Or *"did you [speaking to the circlee] feel gotten by that? What would have helped to make you feel more seen?"*. Or *"I notice that people seem to be giving Joey advice. I wonder what that is about?"*. It creates group safety when you intervene on communications which are distancing or not-related. Plus, it's 90% probable the target of your intervention will be grateful to you. In the unusual event in which they seem upset, ask them if they are okay and circle them around it. Always thank them for gracefully taking your feedback, of course.

- DON'T feel an obligation to be a great leader. Understand that 80% of your job is to witness and affirm, 15% to show vulnerability, and 5% to challenge or redirect. Anybody can witness and affirm, so if you feel stuck, do only that until you get a better idea, or something bubbles up in you that demands to be said.

- DO be humble and trust the process. Gracefully accept any feedback they might give you, even (and especially) if it's negative. If you feel something is off, probe the group for negative impact: *"am I being too bossy or directive here?"* or *"let's do a quick temperature check. Is anyone not present or engaged here, and if so, what could we do that would help?"*. I can guarantee you that will wake them up.
- Remember: *"trust that people move towards wholeness, and we just have to follow"* [Alexis Shepperd].

A/R Game Format

Introductions

I usually start with an introduction round of: (1) *Name*, (2) *Why you are here*, and (3) *Something unique or unusual about you (or: anything you would like the group to know about you)*.

Context-setting

Then I do a brief context-setting, saying something along the lines of:

- To talk about A/R is not actually doing Authentic Relating, so need to keep it brief
- Nonetheless, a little bit of context is helpful
- The best context I have for A/R is this: A/R is the invitation to bring more of ourselves into interaction with people, to stop cloaking our humanity or pretending to be something different than who we really are. To actually have the courage to say things like *"I would love if you could talk less and pay more attention to me"* or *"I just got angry there and realized that you are talking to me like my mother used to do. It's not really about you"*. Etc..
- I tell them we are going to play some communication games, but that it is very important that they don't do anything they don't want to do, or feel any pressure to show up any way other than they are currently feeling. They can sit-out any game and if they have an objection to anything that's going on, they should voice it.

- I almost always give some history, even brief, explaining that the A/R movement started in California (of course!) in 1999 as the Circling practice, which has now spread into "Authentic" communities in 60+ cities, 3 major schools, two online platforms, thousands of people impacted and a very active global community, etc. I also explain that the A/R movement has two primary practices, A/R games and Circling. (there is also a third practice, my favorite actually, [Guerrilla Circling](#) which is circling people invisibly and without agreement, but that's too complex to explain in an intro)
- Finally, I do short "popcorn-style" impacts on my context-setting

Warm-up

Plan on 15-20 minutes for the warm-up and the warm-up impact round (debrief). The warm-up is very important because it tends to "drop" people into connection immediately, and enter a place of presence from which the actual circle will be way more powerful. If you start a circle without a warm-up, it will be more difficult to "drop in" later.

Here is what has worked for me:

- Set them up in pairs. You can do an inner and outer circle (which rotates for the 3 games) or you can just ask them to find a partner. It tends to reduce anxiety if you set a clear structure of who they will be with (i.e. an inner and outer circle, don't give them a choice). If you are doing triad breakouts rather than pairs, have them count-off.
- **I do one round of "best friends" game.** Here is what you tell them: *"First, pick a person to begin. Then, you are going to explain to this person what they would need to know about you to be your best friend. Who you are, what you value and enjoy, what you hate, and all your personality flaws that your best friend would need to know and accept about you. Start now, you have 3 minutes"*. If they seem to be having fun, you can give them a bit more than 3 minutes. Then switch.

- **One round of Noticing Game**. I say: *"Okay so now we are going to get more relational and more present-moment"*. I bring out a participant or my co-lead and I model the process: *"The structure is as follows: First person says 'I notice (bla)'. You could notice something about their physical experience, an emotional reaction you are having to them, or something completely unrelated to them, like your wife is leaving you and you just lost your job and so you are feeling distracted. Second person says: 'On hearing that, I notice (bla)'. And so forth"*. I say: *"This is a one of the basic A/R exercises and you can go wherever you want with it. Specifically, you can go for depth, or you can go for fun and playful, or both"*. I encourage them to move their body (I won't kick them out if they want to do a dance). *"Start now, you have about 4 or 5 minutes for both people to share"*.
- **Then I might switch partners and do a second round of Noticing Game. If the group is strong I change the final Noticing Game to eye-gazing**, telling them: *"Eye-gazing simply honors the fact that connection can happen non-verbally, as a felt experience. You have at least two choices here. You can either send direct love and appreciation non-verbally, or you can just be non-judgmentally aware and appreciative of what arises in the space"*.
- **Then I will do a "popcorn-style" impact round (debrief) on Noticing Game**

The Game

- **Then I give everyone a hot-seat and an appreciation/impact round**. This has worked EXCEEDINGLY well. For instance, in a group of 8 in a 2 hour meeting, each person would get (excluding the introductions, context-setting and checkout) roughly a 7 minute hot-seat and a 3-minute impact/appreciation round (which is a bit short, but it works). My experience is that people understand the meaning of "impacts / appreciations" immediately and provide quite powerful appreciations and reflections to each other. Occasionally (very occasionally) I do a redirect in the impact round, specifically if the impacts start to look like coaching or advice-giving.

- **Here is how I explain the Hot-Seat role**: *they are going to get all of the attention in the room for X minutes (this is why we call it a "hot seat", it can get rather hot to receive all that loving attention!). People will be invited to ask them questions, which they can answer, or not, as they please. Indeed during their hot-seat they are going to be the undisputed King or Queen of the evening.*
- **Here is how I explain the "Questioner" role in Hot-Seat**: *they can ask any question that they have genuine curiosity about, even questions that might seem risque. They should not shut-down or dampen their genuine curiosity, because the person on the hot-seat does not have to answer if they don't want to.* I also tell them that they should say *"Thank you"* when the person finishes talking, OR when they have heard enough. This completes the cycle and we can take another question, either from them or somebody else.

Checkout round

I always end with a checkout round: *"How are you feeling and What are you taking home from this"*

I will be experimenting with another format as well, a 3-hour meeting with a 20-30 minute refreshment and socializing break after the first 1 1/2 hours. This requires snacks which is an added expense, unless you can (ideally) get someone to bring the food. The benefit is that it's hard for people to sustain the intensity of attention for more than 2 hours. Plus they appreciate the informality of the break.

That's it. **I do not have a need to do something different every time (as I see happening sometimes in the A/R game space).** If I find a format that works every time, I will just repeat it until it gets boring to me or I get feedback that the group wants something different.

Circling Introduction Leader Format

In this section I offer a Circling Introduction Leader that has worked very well for me in a group size of between 6 and 10 participants in a 2 hour meeting. If there are more than 9 or 10 people you will, in my experience, need to break-out (so you would need a qualified co-lead).

This approach involves giving people short birthday circles, normally 10 minutes plus a 5 minute impact round. The goal here is to give as many people as possible an experience of being birthday circled (of being the designated circlee) and as many people possible the experience of giving impact statements (being the designated circler). These are the two basic roles of Circling, in my world. Having them formally put in to the structure helps to clarify an important distinction. Short birthday circles can be very powerful, and they also distribute the air-time better.

Alternatives to this are organic circles, SL-style circles, or long birthday circles. My preference as a leader to beginners is to get them excited and enrolled through an initial (and hopefully powerful) experience of being circled, even if it be short. In later groups with people who have gone through the format I am presenting here, you can dispense with all instructions and pre-set structure (other than paired-share warmups) and just flow into an organic circle, a single birthday circle, multiple mini-birthday circles, or whatever you feel the group needs.

I will go now into the precise languaging I use, with the caveat that Circling is a presence practice, so you need to "come from being" rather than a pre-set structure, and to be open to feedback from the group of how you are occurring to them as a leader. If you are leading an A/R Game rather than a Circle, see my A/R Game Leader Format above.

Overall Leadership Guidelines

These are the same guidelines as for the A/R Game Leader Format above. When leading a circle (versus an A/R Game), you can be less inhibited in giving feedback on communications which you judge to be "not connecting" (i.e. you might circle people who make communications that are not real impact statements, such as coaching or advice-giving).

Introductions

You can use the same introduction given in the A/R Game format above.

Context-setting

Then I do a brief context-setting, saying something along the lines of:

- To talk about Circling is not actually doing Circling, so need to keep it brief
- Nonetheless, a little bit of context may be helpful
- **The are many contexts that you can set for a Circle.** If you are leading to mixed beginners and more experienced people (who might have heard your context before), you can vary or rotate among some of the following (or include several of them):
  1. Circling is the invitation to bring more of ourselves into interaction with people, to stop cloaking our humanity or pretending to be something different than who we really are. To actually have the courage to say things like *"I would love if you could talk less and pay more attention to me"* or *"I just got angry there and realized that you are talking to me like my mother used to do. It's not really about you"*. Etc..
  2. Circling is being more deliberate about how we approach relationships. That most of us yearn to connect with people at deeper levels of sharing and truth, and yet we tend to approach relationships with people we care about or that we are interested in, in an overly timid or haphazard way, perhaps achieving success only by accident
  3. Circling is an explicit invitation into having the deeper level of conversation that most of us yearn for, but that few have the courage to ask for directly. Thus, in Circling we will enter into an explicit agreement that it's okay here

to speak from (and listen for) our experience of what it's like to be us, alive in our bodies in this moment
4. Unlike the conversations that happen in bars, at church, at work, and at your average party, we come together in Circling with the explicit desire to know and be known, and permission to express what is true for us, outside of social rules or political correctness
5. Circling is about "being present to what is", especially in the space between us (relational / emotional reality). Listen to Guy Sengstock on this.
6. Make up your own context?

- Then I tell them we are going to play some communication games, but that it is very important that they don't do anything they don't want to do, or feel any pressure to show up any way other than they are currently feeling. They can sit-out any game and if they have an objection to anything that's going on, they should voice it.
- I almost always give some history, even brief, explaining that the A/R movement started in California (of course!) in 1999 as the Circling practice, which has now spread into "Authentic" communities in 60+ cities, 3 major schools, two online platforms, thousands of people impacted and a very active global community, etc. I also explain that the A/R movement has two primary practices, A/R games and Circling.
- Finally, I do short "popcorn-style" impacts on my context-setting. (*"What lands here for you? What dissonates or makes you feel resistant?"*)

Warm-up
You can use the same warm-up as for the A/R game, above

The Circle
- I like to decide in advance how many people will get mini-birthday circles and announce, say: *"we are going to do 4 short birthday circles. A birthday circle is where one person gets all the attention of the group for a certain amount of time"*. Ask who would like to begin, or (better) if

there is someone that piques your interest and attention, say so and ask them if they want to start.
- Time the birthday circle. Try not to go over. You can hold up fingers to indicate how many minutes left (3, 2, 1, 0). Don't worry too much about cutting them off. Trust that they will say what's important to them in the time that they have. Don't be inhibited about imposing structural time-constraints. Most people feel relieved and grateful and that they can relax into a structure that feels safe and fair.
- Time the impact/appreciation round. If necessary give some context of impact/appreciation: *"it's an opportunity to either say something you appreciate about someone, or else a way in which they have affected you, in case you have a felt experience or reaction to them"*. You may need to remind them to keep it brief in view of time constraints.
- Then on to the next.

This is a format that works well for beginner circles. With more advanced circlers, once they get the basic concepts and the vocabulary, you can relax the structure, and you can also probe the group for how much structure they want.

Checkout round

Checkout round is same as for the A/R game.

TIPS FOR GIVING AND RECEIVING FEEDBACK

> *"A trouble shared is a trouble halved. A joy shared is a joy doubled"* – Anonymous

This article is adapted from a handout at Network for a New Culture (www.nfnc.org). See the previous chapter for more information about NFNC.

Why giving feedback is important

When we can't share what's wrong, such as a distressing experience we are having in relation to a person or an organization, small annoyances become deep resentments and we stifle energy that could be put towards creating productive collaborations. And if we are unwilling to receive feedback, we lose out on valuable information about how we come across to others – information that we can use to grow and mature. As resentments fester, organizations suffer with high turnover and low morale, and families and friendships split apart.

The solution to this problem is to adopt a culture where giving and receiving feedback is a regular and non-threatening part of day-to-day life. You can:

1. Work it out directly with the other person, via the process I am about to describe.
2. Ask for help from a third person to help you clarify your emotions prior to the exchange, and/or ask the third person to mediate the meeting.
3. Decide to completely let it go: internally clear the slate with the other person (maybe with some help from a friend or confidante)

All three options can be good, but they all require skill, self-awareness and generosity.

Tips for giving feedback

1. Check-in with yourself: is this the right time? If you are still very upset with the person, or your energy is not the best, you would be wise to speak first with a third person, whom you could ask to listen to you and help you clear as much of the upset as possible before engaging.
2. Ask if the other person is open to receiving feedback and if it's a good time.
3. Be aware of your intentions in giving the feedback. Go forward if you are wanting to get closer to the other person, have better communication, or find a solution to a problem. Feedback with the intention of shaming or pushing the other person usually makes the situation worse.
4. Share your experience, and especially your felt-experience. What were your feelings, thoughts, stories? Give specific examples whenever possible. As much as possible, do not make the other person wrong for how they are behaving. If you share judgments, declare upfront that you know that your judgments may not be "the truth".
5. Be curious about the other person, how you might be impacting them and what they might be thinking. Hint: their experience will rarely be what you imagine it to be.
6. Be clear about what you want to happen, or not happen, in the future. Make a specific request if you can.

Avoid:
1. Name-calling or labeling.
2. Assigning motives to the other person *("you did that because you were jealous")*.
3. Most important: **remember that the point of the feedback is to affect your future with this person in a positive way** – not to achieve catharsis, or correct them for some disrespect or injustice, either real or imagined.

Tips for receiving feedback

1. Check-in with yourself: how is your listening? If you are over-tired, angry or upset, you may want to thank the person

for reaching out to you and tell them that you value your relationship with them, but suggest a "timeout" so that you can give them your best attention later. Ask them if that's okay with them.
2. Reflect back what you heard. This ensures that the other person knows you understand what they are telling you.
3. Ask questions. This helps you learn more and helps the other person know you're interested in what they have to say.
4. Thank the speaker for being willing to give you the feedback. You can even appreciate them for their courage – it may be hard for them to do.
5. Avoid instant judgments of whether the other person is right or wrong. Focus, instead, on the probable reason they are sharing this with you: to get internal clarity for themselves and work through an upset. They may change their mind about you if you just listen to them without arguing or making them wrong. They want the same thing as you do: to be heard. Offer this to them, out of love and respect.
6. After reflecting back, asking questions and thanking them, ask them if it's okay for you to respond, in case you feel moved to. Be willing to honor their "no".

Remember:
1. Feedback that feels "wrong" to you may contain a kernel of truth. Feedback that sounds "right" to you may be only their projection. So, "*take what you like and leave the rest*".
2. This is a golden opportunity to get to know, understand and appreciate the person who is giving the feedback. And who knows, they may become your best friend.
3. **Negative feedback to you doesn't mean there is anything wrong with you!!!**

OTHER BOOKS BY MARC

As Lovers Do: Sexual and Romantic Partnership as a Path of Transformation

As Lovers Do is both a profound analysis of the issues that stop men and women from getting along, *and* a practical guide for creating deeper relationships and having better sex. Starting with the basic idea that men's natural role and deepest desire is to support women, take care of them and attempt to make them happy – an idea that is frequently ridiculed and denied in our post-conventional society, which pretends that men and women are the same – we then review new models and distinctions on sexual relationships which carry the potential to dramatically improve the quality of our intimate relationships, and even to end patriarchy as we know it.

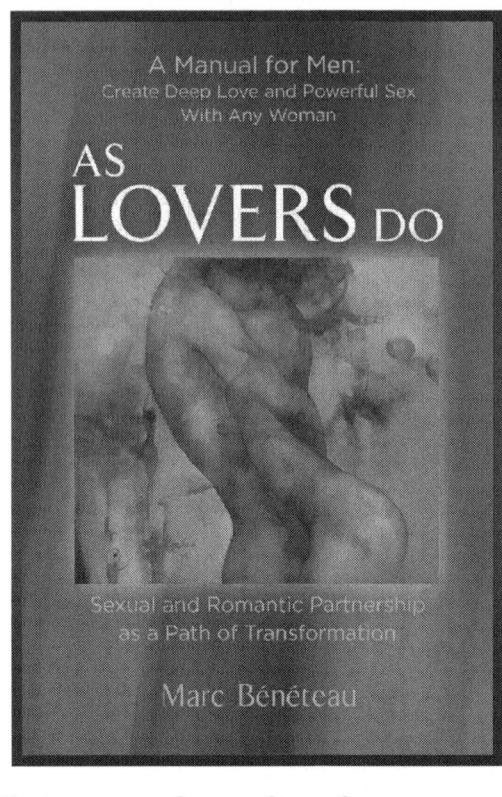

Some of the wise and powerful teachers whose ideas are reviewed are: **Scott Peck** and **Jerry Jud** on human loving; **David Deida**, **Victor Baranco** and **Alison Armstrong** on sexual polarity, sacred sexuality and female orgasm; **Marshall Rosenberg, Dale Carnegie** and **Werner Erhard** on emotional communication; **Mark Manson** and **Steve Bodansky** on sexual attraction and seduction; and **Dieter Duhm** on internalized oppression. Some of these great teachers are still alive, others have passed-on; all of them built significant learning communities; but As Lovers Do is the *only* summary and integration of these powerful ideas into a comprehensive system for understanding man/woman relationships. If you don't know who these teachers are, and why their ideas are important, you are in for an eye-opening experience!

Sexual intimacy is one of the deepest human needs, and yet the one that is most frequently repressed and denied – doubly so as men and women often repeatedly act out self-destructive patterns in pursuit of their sexual and relational needs. We do this, mostly, out of ignorance, attempting to follow social norms that are broken and lead to poor results. In reality, relating powerfully to the opposite sex is a lot easier than most people imagine, once you get the basic ideas which are presented here.

Note: the book is written from a male perspective and therefore should be of particular interest to young men, who are often shockingly and tragically ignorant about women. However there is wisdom here for people of all ages and genders.

A few reviews:

"While the popular culture is still sending couples into "couples counselling" and using the medical model to pathologize one or both members of a couple who are struggling, there has been a plethora of new thought about how to actually SUCCEED at relationship. Mark has been a student of these new pioneers for at least 20 years, and has essentially written THE survey text book about this body of new thought." – Max Rivers, Marriage Counselor & NVC Facilitator

"This book unites some of the best ideas that have been developed by modern day experts in the fields of sexuality and relationship. Marc has chosen the best information from each to enable the reader to evaluate and create a better relationship with a partner, the world and with one's self. He gives you enough time with each master to get the main ideas that they have described, allowing us to delve further if we so wish by including many references. After reading this book I felt better, more aware, more in love and kinder to myself, my lover and to my friends. " – Steve Bodansky, Sex Educator, Bestselling Author of "Extended Massive Orgasm" and 3 other books.

Printed in Great Britain
by Amazon